Hazel,
Beautiful Woman of God,
Continue to walk in purpose
the anointing that God has
life. You've overcome to help others.
Believe. Speak. Manifest your God

10/10/2020

I...Am Chosen

21 Biblical Affirmations & Influential Messages to Develop
Your God-Identity

IG: iAmArnesjah

Arnesjah Miller

I...AM CHOSEN: 21 AFFIRMATIONS & INFLUENTIAL MESSAGES TO DEVELOP YOUR GOD-IDENTITY

This publication and its materials are not intended for use as a source of legal, financial, professional, physical health, or medical advice. As with any business or experience, your results may vary, and will be based on your individual capacity, expertise, and effort. There are no guarantees concerning the results and success you may experience.

Printed in the United States of America

For information on bulk purchases or permission requests, please contact us at:
TransparentTreasure@gmail.com

ISBN: 9781713095019

But ye are chosen…
- 1 Peter 2:9

You cannot remain silent.
Perhaps, you have been chosen
for such a time as this.
- Paraphrase of **Esther 4:14**

Table of Contents

Arnesjah Miller

Fighting for My Identity

Poem

Where do I fall in the category of society?
Who am I to become a woman in authority?
Why did God give me a calling,
Where I am stripped from normality
To become the image that I've been running
Away from, inside of me?

I have unanswered questions
And I feel as though God's not hearing 'em.
I have guidance and lessons
A playlist of messages
Yet, I'm still a hot mess
Trying to walk in confidence...

I'm fighting a war against darkness
And half the time I believe
that something is wrong with me.
My mind morphs into mental monologues
With images of the individuals surrounding me.
I hear death threats and deception
More than I hear God's will for me.

So I, speak life
I meditate on scriptures
I fast and pray through the day
I do my best to starve my flesh
So that I can become more
Of who God is to me.

I...Am Chosen

My flesh is hungry for more than what
The capacity of my spirit can take.
My appetite is longing for more insight
Than what my bare hands can create.

Beloved,
It is written in His Word,
All of your imperfections
And every last one of your questions,
God has given you the wisdom
To overcome them.

He's intended for you to
Discover your identity
Through the lens of His Son
Jesus, the one who overcame
Death and resurrection,
Defeated the kingdom of darkness.
So that you can have life-everlasting
In God's heavenly kingdom.

So, don't worry about what
Tomorrow may bring.
Don't worry about what
your sorrows may breed.
God has already written your story
All for His glory for you to live free
In your God-given identity.

Introduction

Arnesjah, what do you truly want to do in your life?
If you could make a living from your passion, what would that be?
What is your occupation?
What do you aspire to be in life?

I was asked one of these questions four times from four different individuals before I asked God to close the door to my full-time, well-paying job, if it was no longer His will for me. Then next thing I knew, I was fired…

I was a little flustered about being jobless all over again. This meant trusting in God the challenging way. This meant going through the fire to come out as pure as gold. It meant being stripped from my comfort zone all over again, as if I didn't experience this phase two years ago. Was He going to take my new apartment away too? Is God revocable? He wouldn't. After all of the places I've lived in Georgia - twelve different places to lie my head, one including my car, why would He allow me to obtain victory just to take it away? I wouldn't know where else to go. I'd look like a fool losing my job *and* my apartment. God, why?

I spent frequent nights in prayer, overwhelmed with anxious thoughts, dealing with the mental weight of inadequacy due to the lack of open doors in my life. I hated that I was chosen, to be honest. A part of me understood why God predestined my life a special way. However, the other part of me did not want to receive His will. I was resentful towards God within, yet I covered it with a smile publicly. I spent nights emotionally frustrated, worrying about my finances. I was angry at the fact that I was financially barren, unable to receive money when I wanted. I'd pray against poverty. Yet, poverty seemed to be winning the battle.

Somehow, a sudden peace came over me one night. God reminded me that He is the Great I Am. He is Elohim. He is my Provider. I had finally sat silence and allowed God to remind me of how He opened the door for me to get my apartment. During an arduous season I had no choice but to move out of my

4

friends' living room. There was no other apartment fitting for me. Above all, He was the one who just so cogently called me to live in Georgia to inherit my Promised Land, granting me over five confirmations to prove it. So, why was I in worry? He was calling me into a challenging season that required me to be confident that God was up to something greater than I could imagine. All I needed to do was trust in Him and Him alone.

After my last day as an Office Manager of a global staffing company, I'm not gonna lie, I kicked my feet up, hung out with friends, and slept in for the following three days. I'd gotten the most relief out of the hard work that I placed within that job. I knew that God was calling me to another level in Him, which meant I was going to have to focus on my God-given gifts and talents. My weekdays were going to consist of laboring in the Spirit so that I may produce effective results. I would have to pray and fast frequently in order for God to produce the most out of me. I sensed He was manifesting greatness out of my circumstance. Had I lingered in depression or allowed my loss to defeat me, I would have never followed God's will to produce more out of my God-ordained assignments.

This book that you are reading - I...Am Chosen – was derived from an encounter where I was reminded of my identity in Christ Jesus. I was chosen to perform poetry at a Christian talent show hosted by Lifeway Talent. God told me to perform a poem that I'd written in 2014, I...Am. I hadn't performed poetry in about a year. There was something about my poem that reactivated my calling and purpose in God. It brought back memories of why I am chosen by God. It sent chills all over me, serving as a reminder of the power that is within my voice as a poet. It made me wonder what my life would hold if I made poetry my lifestyle again. It was a silent siren of God calling me to another place in Him.

I...Am Chosen is not just a book. I...Am is not only a poem. I...Am is not only a movement. I...Am is my birthright. I...Am is my identity birth into life. It is who God has predestined me to be. I've written influential messages for those who are either struggling to discover their God-identity or are wrestling to accept their God-identity. I Am, the statement alone is powerful. I speak "I Am" biblical affirmations daily and boy is there power in words! I've noticed myself become the very words that I proclaim each day. I encourage you to always remember to be mindful of who you say you are because it will more than likely come to pass.

I've written I...Am Chosen: 21 Affirmations & Influential Messages to Develop Your God-Identity to ignite the power of God's purpose in your life. I've written this book so that the people who truly feel driven to develop into the greatest version of themselves may understand the importance of living in their God-identity. **Your God-identity is defined as your uniquely developed identity within God; to become God's likeness through the lifestyle of Jesus Christ.** It is who God created you to become since the moment you were born into this world. It is your purpose, the answer to your calling. This book is for those who are unsure about their identity or need help walking it out confidently. I believe that the words written within this book will not only influence you, but to also stir up the passion to believe in yourself and to become all of who God created you to be.

I...Am Chosen is also for every Creative battling with mental breakdowns due to the tension of life's expectations to live outside of the ordinary status quo. As you read this book, affirm yourself with who God says you are through His living and true Word. Build a divine covenant with our Father. For it is in Him that you live, move, and have your being; you are his offspring (Acts 17:28). It is within The Great I Am that you will discover your God-identity.

I Was Fired to Pursue My Purpose

Periodically, I have conversations with friends, family, and strangers discussing the topic of purpose. Some of them know their purpose. While some unfortunately do not. Majority of the people that I talk with are aware of the vision to where they ultimately desire to be in life. Yet, they find themselves in a rut, seeking to take the necessary steps toward their destiny. We often hear, *"Work your 9 to 5 then come home to work on your dream."* I was once there. Working to earn money that only left me with enough to pay my bills and necessities. I had to work overtime to earn funds for pleasure.

I've always sensed that working a corporate job would be temporary for my life. As if God was signaling me to pursue something greater, I often dealt with the anticipation the day I'd either get fired or God would call me to quit. It's the lifestyle of a chosen one. We know we are destined for something greater than our current reality. Our inner-man is constantly evolving while our human nature is fighting to keep up. This sensation causes us to seek deeper into discovering how to get to step C before we've even figured out how to accomplish steps A and B.

We live in a world where we can either stand-in with the crowd that tells us how we should live, or we can embrace our indifferent identity and stand-out from the crowd. You can either blend in with familiarity, or you can crowd-surf upon your wildest dreams within your God-identity. It's your choice. We live in a society where we gain the experience and benefits of our corporate jobs that can haphazardly lay us off at any given moment. There are people who plainly surviving. There are others who are fighting for promotion to climb a ladder of success that is under someone else's corporation. There are people who are indeed successful in their corporate position, which is great! I'm not knocking anyone who works a corporate job. But what I want you to realize is the control that you really have when it comes to your job. What happens when your boss tells you that he or she no longer needs your service? What happens when the adrenaline of hope in your job position dies off? Where do you go when you are stuck with questions, fears, doubts, and frustrations? How will you make ends meet? Do you have a plan after lay-off? Is there life after lay-off? I can attest that there is.

I remember the time when my former boss called me to speak with her in our office's meeting room. She and another co-worker were in the room where they'd just ended an important business call. She welcomed me to take a seat at the table. For a moment, I thought she was going to correct me about something I'd probably did wrong again. Perhaps I should've had the conference call ready for her. Or, maybe she was going to correct my frustration with her blaming me for the failed connection with her important conference call. In that moment, I just had enough of feeling unqualified. Sure enough, that was the problem. She told me that she no longer needed my services and that I was unqualified for the position. Hearing her tell me that actually made me feel relieved.

I sunk in the moment of my reality. My response to my boss's lay-off notice was, "I agree." By her expression, she seemed surprised. I explained to her why I felt as if I didn't qualify for the position. I also let her know what I felt was more fitting for me. She suggested other jobs within the company but I denied them. I didn't want to live in another Jonah experience. I knew that God was in control of my life. Had I stepped outside of God's will, it could likely cause the ship to sink.

The pressure of my job was getting real. I wrestled all 90 business days with the dying urge to leave the job that I knew was not fitting for me. I was extremely determined to stick out the hustle. God beckoned me to let it go. But I needed provision. I didn't want to give in to the lifestyle of poverty that was seemingly knocking at my back door. I desired to embrace my blessings. I hated being broke. Why did contentment seem to impoverish me? Before my boss broke the news to me, I was in a co-worker's office weeping because I felt as if our boss didn't recognize my over-achieving efforts. I was working in a whirl-wind trying to coordinate the company's annual meeting perfectly to the T while dealing with other complications and setbacks on the job. I strived for everything to be in place flawlessly because I anticipated rejection.

It was within the last two weeks of working my job that I accepted my loss. I needed to lose the job to gain a more excellent vision that God wanted to fulfill in my life. If He said that Atlanta is my Promised Land, then it was best that I strapped up and accepted it full circle. The very last day on the job, my boss expressed to me how she acknowledged my hard work and energy that I placed within the role. She said, "Normally, people wouldn't remain the last two weeks." She decided to compensate me for the final two weeks in July even after my last day of work. It was totally an unexpected blessing.

I currently live in Atlanta. Thankfully, I'm still in my one-bedroom apartment that I feared would be taken away from me. It's the God-honest truth when I tell you that it is not easy to find a job in Atlanta. The population is so high that you have to compete to find the job you want. You're blessed if you know someone who can get you a job opportunity. Atlanta is a city filled with entrepreneurs. It's filled with opportunities to help you pursue your purpose. It is solely up to you to know when to seize perfect opportunities. It is up to you to believe in yourself. It is up to you to develop your craft. It is up to you to make an impact where you are. It is ultimately up to you to think wisely of how to build a legacy for your family and for future generations.

Arnesjah Miller

Identity Crisis

I feel very strongly about expressing my views about identity. There is a fire arising within me. I'm asking God, *"What is truly within me that I can give to the world?"* I can feel this unbearable anger stretching as my imagination widens to the deep concerns about the lack of confidence within my peers. On the other hand, I realize that many are on the pursuit of purpose without healing and fully developing their spirit to withstand the journey. I've run into an identity crisis, fighting with man's titles, yet I'm reading my Bible to discover that I am who God says I am.

I'm beaten down by gravity, constantly fighting the enemy for the sake of rescuing a pool of crippled Creatives. I love producing creative ideas and teaching people about God. But every now and then, I suddenly come to a breaking point where everything within me falls to pieces. As if the fuel of the fire of God no longer flows rivers of living water to fill the empty cups of the thirsty. As if my burdens in life constantly suck the oxygen out of my spirit. I pause, and then I yearn to break away from the people that need insight on how to follow after the King. Lord knows it's not easy to live in God-identity.

We live in a day and age where there are various systems that teaches us how to discover our purpose. We have multiple streams of prosperous entrepreneurs, influencers, MUA's, and other creative individuals. They've given us the tools, their testimonies, their ideas all with the purpose of helping us acclimate to a higher level. But what happens when we've watched all of the videos, read majority of the books, read hundreds of emails, and invested in their webinars and conferences, yet we are still battling with an identity crisis?

You may be asking God in this very moment,
"Who am I?"
"How am I supposed to live in my purpose?"
"What is my purpose?"
"Why am I frustrated with my job?"
"Where am I truly supposed to fit in within the industry?"

We hear the saying all the time, "What do you believe you are purposed to do?" To avoid all appearances of uncertainty, we beat around the bush to sound like we've got it all together. We simply answer, "An entrepreneur." Their response is something like, "Oh, an entrepreneur! How do you plan to make that work out? Entrepreneurship is not an easy job, you know. Entrepreneurs usually don't make a living to begin with." Here we go with the common doubtful remarks. It seems like all of the non-entrepreneurs have all of the *advice* to give us, yet they haven't stepped out of their comfort zone to pursue entrepreneurship. They may be correct about the difficulty of starting off an entrepreneurial business. However, they don't know that you were specifically built for entrepreneurship. They don't know that the calling on your life is meant to make an incredible impact on the world. They don't acknowledge that you are chosen.

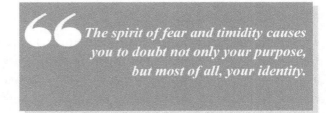

The spirit of fear and timidity causes you to doubt not only your purpose, but most of all, your identity.

If you believe that you have the ideas, the skills, and the strategies for a sector within the entrepreneurship industry, you must also believe in yourself to fulfill the assignment. You must disengage with the opinions and fears from man. This goes for anything that you believe you are called to pursue. How will you respond in the face of the fear of man? Let's talk about this fear that many of us Creatives fight with at times. Fear is indeed a spirit that God has not given you. For it is written in 2 Timothy 1:7 *"God has not given you a spirit of fear and timidity, but of power, love, and sound mind."* In other words, God has made you fearless with capabilities to soar in the identity that He has given you within the Spirit of power, love, and a sound mind.

Who would have known how much fear would have an impact of isolating you from your God-identity? Fear will try to make you timid of God's amazing plans for your life. Did you know that when you are fearful of your God-identity, you are rejecting God's image of you? He gave His life through Christ Jesus for a specific purpose - to save mankind from the sins of this world; to redeem mankind with Himself; to give mankind life and life more abundantly. He's given you purpose as well. Many believers have become victims to fear. The spirit of fear has instilled a false reality within our imagination, causing us to lose faith in God's purpose for our lives. Whether you were raped as a child and it caused you to believe that you were meant to be homosexual. Whether God gave you a prophetic vision of your future and you didn't believe you could make it that far in life. Whether you've been through enough trials in the pursuit of your purpose and you threw in the towel. Or maybe you just don't know who you are…period. The spirit of fear will use your vulnerability in any of these areas to attempt to prevent you from living in your God-given purpose.

Trust me, I've questioned God plenty of times about my identity. Since then, He's pulled out every version of myself to the point where I have too many hats to wear. One day I'm a poet; the next day, I'm either an entrepreneur or an evangelist. In one season, I'm a missionary. Another season I'm working for someone's company. In this very moment of my life, I'm quite a bit overwhelmed with my decision to either pursue my ministry Transparent Treasure, pursue my business Prayer Mats by Arnesjah, or launch everything at one time.

The protocol to the entrepreneurial world says to start with one idea and go forth. I agree that it is easier to launch one name and one business at one time. However, with me being a Creative with multiple ideas flowing out of me at once, it's a challenge to focus on one thing. I am an author, a poet, an influencer, and an entrepreneur fighting to maintain one hat at a time. Let alone, I'm in the process of deciding how to present myself to people. Should I let everyone know that I'm Aesthete Nesjah, or am I Arnesjah? Blah! I love my artist name Aesthete Nesjah! It has a deeper meaning and purpose as to who I am. What makes it humorous is that people can hardly pronounce it...*sigh...I decrease...I can sense the Lord telling me that my birth name, Arnesjah, is just enough to bring Him glory.

Running away from your identity is just as equivalent to running away from your purpose. I feel led to talk to the homosexual or the one who has overcome homosexuality. To the woman who is running with the identity of a man. I want to reach out to you. You do not have to reject your identity as a woman in the pursuit of finding love. I understand what it is like to believe that you're a boy because of this internal turn-on that you have with women. It feels as if you were born to like women. You think God mistakenly created you to be a woman. But all of those assumptions are not true.

At a very young age, the spirit of homosexuality rested within me. I thought that it was normal for me to dress like a tomb-boy. I thought that it was normal to see the nudity of women. For as long as I could, I've tried to remove the memory of the happenstance of me being played with by a female family member, which to my understanding made me comfortable with liking other girls. Up until the age of 18 I held on to my secret of wondering why I liked a certain type of women. I didn't want anyone to know because I knew that people would reject me. Lord knows the amount of rejection I'd face had I told my family members. I didn't know how to get the feeling out of me. So, I kept telling God, "I don't know why lustful thoughts come to my mind when I'm around certain females. Please take it away!"

Though I desired to be in love with a man more than anything, I still had the possibility of having a female partner behind closed doors. What made me turn away from the spirit of homosexuality was when I gave my life to Christ...completely. There came a time where I had a life-changing encounter with God which caused me to surrender my life to Jesus. He began to rebuild my life for Him from the ground up. God revealed to me that His desire was for me to be a leader of a community, married to a man of God, and to give birth to a powerful generation. Had I run with the lie that I was supposed to be a male, I would have never believed in my purpose to help other women to develop their identity and to pursue their purpose in Christ.

Becoming a woman of my God-identity has not been a beautiful bed of roses and green grass on the other side. Communing with females has always been a hardship for me. It truly feels like a generational curse that I've been called to demolish. Ever since I was a child, I've had issues with getting along with my mother. Let alone, let's not forget the rivalries I'd have at school and afterschool care. I didn't have a trustworthy relationship with my female teachers and I hardly made any long-term friends. I often felt like the odd ball in a group of kids, which made it frustrating to accept my identity.

From Elementary School to Middle School, I've dealt with a terrible case of an identity crisis. You may think that as a kid, you don't really know who you are. However, your instinct knows that feeling mistreated, rejected, or unnoticed is not a good feeling. I dealt with anger issues not knowing how to express myself while trying to figure out why trouble always seemed to find me. If only you could imagine being the one girl that everyone looked at as a problem. The one girl who was always bullied, sent to the principal's office, separated in time out because she was labeled as a trouble-maker. The one girl whom people assumed to be the problem-child. That was my identity for my entire childhood.

During my High School years, thank God trouble didn't follow me as it did in my previous years. The only trouble that I dealt with was drama of not knowing who to share personal information with or who was truly my friend. I can say that while I was in High School, I had more trouble at home than I did at school. Long story short, while I was in 8th grade, my dad married a woman who was not quite fitting to be a step-mother to me. There was always division between the two of us, which seemed to worsen as I grew older.

She'd manipulate me by setting up plots to create a fight between the two of us. She'd make childish remarks to diminish my personality. When my dad wasn't present in the home, she'd set me up to create a physical fight. Every time I'd step up for myself, I was the one who is in the wrong. Do you know how frustrating it is to live with constant beat-downs, drama, and restriction for a good seven years? I wouldn't wish that lifestyle on anyone. Thank God I no longer have to deal with that chapter of my life! I truly hope and pray that wherever she is in life that she is healed and in a much better place.

I express all this to state that the trouble of my childhood left an impact on my identity. It has marked me with unanswered questions that followed up with me until my adulthood. You may have the same questions as I:

"Why do I have to live my life this way?"
"Why am I constantly viewed as a problem or a burden?"
"When do the cycles of drama end?"
"How does all of this fit into my purpose?"
"When will my relationships with people get better?"
"When will I finally see God's promises come to pass?"

I feel you in every last one of these questions. I am determined to let you know that it gets better. There are levels to your deliverance. Depending on how deeply rooted the spirits of rejection, fear of man, or homosexuality has been festering in your life, it can take a little while longer for you to settle down and allow God to work on your wholeness. All of the trials that you face with people can cause you to question your God-identity. But once you genuinely walk out your freedom from the questions that you have towards your identity and accept your God-given purpose, you'll then become unstoppable in the Kingdom of God.

You see, I have constantly felt rejected by females, and because of this rejection, I felt comfortable hanging with guys throughout my High School and young adult years. It was something about men that made me feel accepted, wanted, or entertained. When I accepted my God-given identity, that is where the tables turned. I had to get rid of my male friends while God positioned me around mostly females within my church. It seemed as if God had taken away the heavy weight of troubles that the enemy caused in my female friendships. Though there are some moments where problems attempt to arise to create separation between a friend and me, I recognize the spirit operating in the problem first and I seek God on how to handle the problem. I'm reminded that it is not flesh and blood that I am fighting against, but against the evil principalities of darkness (Ephesians 6:12).

I encourage you to seek God on behalf of the relationships in your life and how they play a role in your identity. There could be people around you who are crippling your confidence as pursue your purpose. There could also be others who desire the best for you. Seek the Lord regarding the thoughts that you have towards yourself. If you oftentimes think negative thoughts, it is likely due to thoughts that you've held on to from the past. When you feel negatively towards yourself and the people in your life, it is a sign that you have not been completed in the love of God and this could very much hinder you from progressing in your purpose.

Identity Comparison

When you're chosen, you are unique – one of a kind. The Greek word for chosen is *eklektos* which means select by implication favorite, elect; chosen out by God for the rendering of special service to Him. I can surely attest to this definition. I've fought long and hard to stand firm in my calling as a chosen child of God. This calling can get rough. Life seems unfair at times. Heck, I've compared myself with others, wishing that I could live my free-spirited-happy-go-lucky self in my own little world. I've come to realize that my identity is IMPOSSIBLE to escape. So, what do you do when you want to live outside of the means of your being? God has told me to tell you to *embrace* your identity, beloved.

> *Running from your identity as a chosen one can tempt you to compare yourself to someone else's walk, even though you are certain that the identity you withhold is incomparable.*

Man's Comparison versus God's Comparison

I've looked from the outside of others to the inward, hidden places of their soul to find that comparison is a trap of fantasies filled with fluff. The more we dwell on becoming something we are not, the more we are influenced to step outside of the will of God. If we make any comparison, it would be best to compare our fruit with the fruit of the Spirit. You see, there is a difference between man's doing of comparison versus God's comparison. Man often compares to either provoke competition or pressure into popularity. On the other hand, God compares us for the benefit of becoming more like Him. I love how Jesus teaches us in such a picturesque way of how God examines our hearts. He cuts off branches [of our heart] that does not bear fruit [of the Spirit], and He prunes the branches that bear fruit so that we can bear even more [richer and finer] fruit (John 15:2, emphasis added).

In the case of God cutting off and pruning branches within me, that lets me know that He is comparing my heart (in the right way) with His expectations of my life. I'm reminded of 1 Samuel 16:7, where it states, *"People look at the outward appearance, but the LORD looks at the heart."* Not only does God look at our heart, but throughout the entire Bible, He desires for us to walk in His ways as His chosen daughters and sons. We stand out for a divine purpose, to represent His glory. Therefore, we must walk in His ways, bearing the fruit of the Spirit. We walk in His ways, of course, by remaining in Him. As we remain in Him – praying, fasting, and studying His Word – we reflect Him upon the earth. We are demonstrating the power and works of His glory.

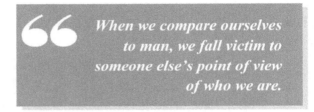

When we compare ourselves to man, we fall victim to someone else's point of view of who we are.

It doesn't matter what man thinks about you. God sees you as His chosen child. His daughter or His son, who carries a unique identity and is a force to be reckoned with. I encourage you to strip off the comparison clothes that your mom, dad, relatives, friends, co-workers, church family, and strangers have donated to you and exchange it with the armor of GOD! Comparison has weighed you down with chains of bondage. It has entangled you with confusion, doubt, fear, insecurity, falsies - false assumptions, false burdens, and false expectations – that God has not promised you. I see that you've lived in a fog, wandering in the same place, listening to people tell you how you should live your life. Even in your own church home. People that you've looked up to have stared you in the eye to encourage you, but behind closed doors, they've ridiculed your potential. The people you thought were your friends have lied on you, turned their backs against you, and left you alone feeling abandoned. There are times where you've accepted your loneliness. But that loneliness leaves your bitter, wishing to come out of a forbidden cave.

Abba Father has not given me the desire to write this book for my own good. I truly believe that He wants to reach you right where you are. It doesn't matter if you're entangled in filthy rags. It doesn't matter how much you've sinned. He's not even turning against you because of your sin-cycles. The fact that you've acknowledged that you need help and you're finding a way to seek Him, He rejoices over you. The eyes of your heart need to be enlightened so that you may be able to sense, feel, hear, know, and delight in the reckless love of God.

You've run your credit card bills up the wall of China, trying to look as good as the people you admire. You've doubted every idea and opportunity that was sent your way due to past traumatic experiences with people-hurt. You've sat too long in the fire of fear of failure, afraid that people aren't going to accept you because of your peculiarity. I tell you the God honest truth, if you can relate to any of what you've just read, I will be open and honest to tell you that I've lived through the lenses of what I've just shared with you. Comparison has left me with nothing but broken, bitter bruises that leads me right back into the arms of our Heavenly Father. He always reminds me that no matter how hard I try to figure my life out, I am a Creative with a unique identity. Chosen to do good works for His glory. He wouldn't have taken me through my experiences for nothing. I've come out of some deep and dark places to help teach you how to live, survive, and rejoice in your identity as His chosen one.

Gifted for Greater

I believe that the enemy influences you to compare our identity with someone whom you weren't meant to be due to a lie that was told to you at a young age. You were called one or more of these hurtful words – weird, ugly, stupid, a loner, odd, strange, unwanted, fat, skinny, the list goes on. These words left permanent scars in your heart because you felt they were true. You knew you didn't fit in, and since that bully called you a hurtful word, you believed it. Those words have resonated within your spirit for quite some time. Like a tattoo's permanent scar, these harmful encounters have blended itself within your identity. It's unfortunate that you have become the very thing that you don't want to be. You've wondered, "How can I change?" Well, there's only one way to change. Change occurs when you surrender your pain to God and allow Him to process you for your greater purpose.

I remember my childhood like it was yesterday. It was the most impactful time of my life, where I experienced the most trauma in regard to my identity. I was bullied, and I bullied kids and adults back. I was bitter. My mom and I didn't have the best relationship. Much healing was needed in our family. I did not fit in with most kids. I forced friendships that never really worked. I was secretly suicidal – constantly wishing I was never born. I deeply desired to be loved. My dad's wife at the time was abusive to me. My dad did little to nothing to truly stand up for me. I just remember desiring to escape home – my real home and my physical being – because it felt as if I didn't belong in the world.

What's crazy is that now that I've given my life to God to accept Jesus as my Lord and Savior, I'm living out this Christian faith-walk. As I'm living it out, I've discovered my purpose. I now realize that all I experienced as a child was used to shape my calling. I didn't know that my indifference to the world was because I am chosen – gifted with the Lord's anointing. All of the dreams and nightmares occurred because I have the gift of discernment. Darkness attempted to keep me bound in anger. The spirit of perversion has tried to taint my purity. The enemy has suffocated my finances because the spirit of poverty doesn't want me to succeed. I could go on with the strongholds that I've had to fight. But I want you to get a clear understanding of why you are gifted.

"The weapons of our warfare are not carnal, but might through God to the pulling down of strongholds."
2 Corinthians 10:4 KJV

I believe that there is a divine revelation that God is waiting for you to accept within your identity if you haven't already. Here's what I want you to do. I want you to take a good look at your past. Reflect on all the encounters that have left a permanent blemish on your identity. Some of these encounters have sat with you for so long that you've become immune to the pain. Perhaps you were sexually assaulted at a young age. Or maybe you were sprung on an uncontrollable addiction. Or, you may have experienced so much rejection that you rejected your own gender. Perhaps, you desperately wanted the attention of the opposite sex so much that you went out of your way to make them want you. Any of these matters could have led you to compare yourself with others. However, God has a gift within you. An anointing. A greater purpose than you can imagine. It is only a matter of time where God will release His promise to fulfill His glory through you. But before God releases His glory through you, you must *authentically* accept your identity in Christ. Accepting your God-identity signals God letting Him know that you are willing to make yourself available to make an impact on this earth. The people that God desires to impact through you are seeking for help, the answers, the strategy, and the presence of God dwelling within you. Will you do away with comparison to accept your identity in Christ?

Arnesjah Miller

Identity Confidence

The beauty of living in your identity is that you've accepted the calling over your life. In accepting your calling, you are breaking the barriers upon someone else's life. I've accepted that one part of my identity is intercession. I know this because I realize that the impact that I have on others through my prayers is uniquely powerful. Quite often, when I pray for people, they tell me that the prayer was right on time, or it was very prophetic, or it impacted their life. Within my personal life, I've seen my prayers shift and break strongholds that I've battled. Often, God lays burdens on me to pray for someone. Even if the circumstances seem uncomfortable, God will not leave me alone until I pray for them. There could be a specific need that an individual requires, and God has chosen me out of the many people within that person's life to allow a miracle to manifest.

A perfect Biblical example of a man who was confident to follow God in an uncomfortable manner was Ananias. Ananias is found in the book of Acts. He was a disciple of what they called *The Way* in his day and age, which is called Christianity today. While Saul (a.k.a. Paul) was on the road to Damascus with a plot to kill believers of Jesus, he had a life-changing encounter with God. God revealed Himself to Saul by striking him down with a bright light, which caused him blindness for three days. Saul was then led to Judas' house (not Judas, the disciple of Jesus) where he began to pray. God had given Saul a vision of Ananias laying hands on him so that he might receive sight again. The Lord visited Ananias to tell him to go and lay his hands on Saul. Ananias reminded the Lord that he has heard about Saul's intent to kill believers of Jesus. Right here is where many of us question God about a life-risking assignment He calls us to. But the Lord told Ananias to go anyway because Saul is a *chosen vessel* to bear His name before Gentiles, kings, and children of Israel (Acts 9:15). Ananias obediently visited Saul to heal him. I believe that Ananias was confident in his God-given identity. He risked his life to respond to his assignment from the Lord. Had he sat around questioning whether it was the Lord speaking to him or his own thoughts, he would have missed out on the opportunity to heal Saul. Let me tell you this, God would never stop you from carrying out His desire and will especially if it relates to someone receiving salvation.

Reading this passage of scripture gave me the revelation that our obedience to answer the call of our God-given identity can unlock blessings for others. This is why it is not only essential to be confident in who God created you to be, but it is imperative to accept the calling on your life. No one else was called to heal Saul besides Ananias. God saw that it was fitting for Ananias to lay hands on Saul. God could have chosen Peter, Phillip, or another disciple. But since Ananias was in position with a willing heart, he was confident in the miraculous work that God was calling him to perform. God called Ananias, gave him instructions, and expected him to carry out His plan. It was Ananias' obedience to God's call that miraculously demolished the barrier that was hindering Saul from living in his new identity. Saul finally received the Holy Spirit and regained his sight. He then was able to live in his identity as a chosen one of God.

You will never know the breakthrough that is waiting for someone else on the other side of your obedience. Your calling will seem unrealistic. It may even require you to make a sacrifice. Remember that your life is not your own. What God has assigned for you is for you because He sees that you are fit for the assignment. You have a divine place to tread upon. Are you willing to stop wrestling, second-guessing, and shying away? I encourage you, my friend, walk in your God-identity with confidence. Pick up that pen and write. Order that camera to start taking pictures and filming. Go back to the book you were working on and finish. Start preparing strategy, business owner. Practice speaking fluently. Go evangelize to people, Evangelist. Speak boldly about what God is saying for His people, Prophet. Keep praying and believing on behalf of God's people, Intercessor. Start gatherings at your home or at the park, Minister. You know who you are and what you are called to do. It is time to get in tune with the purpose and plans of God. Perhaps you were chosen for a time such as this.

Special Message to My Readers

I've written this book with the desire for you to not only be encouraged by the words that God has given to me for you but also to *implement* the Word of God into your daily life. God works wonders when we believe. He works even greater wonders when we act on our faith. When you read and meditate upon these 21 messages, please also do your soul a huge favor to *apply* what is given to you. You've asked for the how-to, the why, the when, the what, the where, and it's here before you. God is always speaking, giving your answers to your prayers. It's now your turn to be still, listen carefully, and activate your faith.

I challenge you to take 21 days to discipline your body, soul, and mind to become a better version of yourself. I personally witness the difference in my life when I decree and declare "I...Am" affirmations. Even more, I feel the presence of God when I sit silently to meditate on scripture for about 30 minutes to an hour. I get excited when I see the manifestation of the results of my prayers. I'd love for you to give it a try.

Prepare yourself to become more like God through Christ Jesus, chosen one. He has special heights that He wants to mount you upon. Receive this moment and don't look back.

21 I…Am
Affirmations & Messages

I...Am Loved
Receiving God's Inseparable Love

Romans 8:38-39 NKJV

For I am fully persuaded that neither death nor life, nor angels nor principalities nor powers, nor things present nor things to come, nor height nor depth, nor any other created thing, shall be able to separate us from the love of God which is in Christ Jesus our Lord.

Love is such a powerful word depending on how it is used. When you say "I am loved," how does it make you feel? Maybe you're wondering who loves you. Perhaps you're thinking, "Am I truly loved?" Beloved, I come to tell you that yes, you are loved and this unconditional love comes from Father God.

During the beginning of my walk with Jesus, I didn't quite understand His love for me. I was trained more so on the practices, discipline, order, and servitude of religion rather than discovering God's love. I was very interested in learning about God's end-times wrath and the apocalypse. Through those studies, I developed a fear of the Lord. I desire to learn more about God and the Bible, so those were the things I sought after. Upon being planted in an African Methodist Episcopal Church for about two years, I grew an understanding of leadership and community service. But God's love for me didn't grasp my soul until I learned the true meaning of trusting entirely in Him in every area of my life. This discovery of God's love occurred once I tapped into my God-identity through Christ Jesus. All of this occurred when I stepped into another level of faith. God brought me to another level of faith where I was stripped from my comfort zone to move to Georgia on my own.

My first move to Georgia was in June 2016. It was the beginning of my Wilderness Season. Which meant that I'd be living a little scarce just for God to reveal Himself as my absolute Provider. It meant living through a discomforting spiritual transition for God to reveal Himself as my Lord. It meant stripping away an old religious mentality and recognizing another dimension of God as the illogical-spontaneous-reckless-loving Heavenly Father. My wilderness was a time where I needed God the most. I spent day after day trying to figure out how to trust God through the unknown. I was searching for a place to live every month because the places that were provided for me were temporary.

Before I moved to Georgia, I had three prophetic dreams where God revealed to me that I'd be living in Atlanta Georgia homeless or in great need. I was never homeless to the extent of the homeless on the street corners. But I was constantly unstable and in great need of provision. My dreams frightened me. It was one of the reasons I wrestled to move. I knew God was calling me to

Arnesjah Miller

move because I felt it in my spirit and I also received numerous biblical messages regarding moving from my home town to a foreign land.

It was as if I couldn't run away from God's call. After finally deciding to take a leap of faith, God actually showed up for me. He continually showed me his unforsaken love through Heaven-sent strangers who were willing to help supply my needs. Some of the people that I met welcomed me into their homes. Some gave me money. And I even met new friends who were walking the same path as me. All of God's provisions proved that I wasn't crazy for trusting Him and I most certainly wasn't alone.

You may be experiencing a wilderness season in your life where you desperately need God. Maybe you're unsure of why you feel set apart. Just because you are experiencing life a little more challenging than others doesn't mean God loves you any less. He is actually stretching your capacity so that you can obtain greater measure in your next season. Our Heavenly Father shows His love for you though disciplined times quite often. He disciplines those He loves.

My son, do not despise the LORD's discipline, and do not resent his rebuke, because the LORD disciplines those he loves, as a father the son he delights in.
Proverbs 3:11-12 NIV

Through it all, God reveals His love through daily encounters. Through radical movements where He shows up through unexpected moments. There are times where a someone provides prayer when you need it the most. He shows His love when He lays it on a stranger's heart to pay for your meal. He shows His love for you even when you backslide. He pulls you out of that situationship, places you on the right track, and positions you to overcome your sin-cycles. God reveals His love for you when you open the Bible and are led to a scripture that aligns with your life. God reveals His love for you when He answers your prayers.

It is never wrong to acknowledge God's love. A sign that reveals you're unaware of God's love is when you are struggling to find your identity. When

28

you're looking for love in all the wrong places, or striving to be someone you're not, or comparing yourself to others, you're misunderstanding God's love for you. If you're struggling to accept God's love for you, how can you love yourself? If you don't know to love yourself, how can you accept your identity? And if you don't accept your identity, how can you genuinely love others?

1 John 4:16 tells us, "God is love, and all who live in love live in God, and God lives in them." This is why you must know who God is - so that you can live in love, and God can live in you. When you get to know God for yourself, you learn about His love not only for you, but for the entire world. As you build your relationship with God, He will give you insight about your identity. Knowing who you are is the best place of freedom you could ever live.

God knew you before you were in your mother's womb. He loved you enough to send His Son so that he could physically demonstrate The Way - a lifestyle of freedom, peace, and authority over the evil principalities in this world. God's love is within you. It's time for you to dig deep and find it. Once you've found His love, dwell in it. Become His love. Share His love. Watch His love come back to you. Receive His love…God has given you all that you need to find Him. All you must do is acknowledge Jesus as Lord and accept Him into your heart. Then you will unlock the door to the unending mystery, miracles, and wonder that is found in Christ. He's showing you the way to God's love right now. Do you receive His love today?

Arnesjah Miller

I...Am Virtuous
Living in Moral Excellence

2 Peter 1:5-8 NKJV

"But also for this very reason, giving all diligence, add to your faith virtue, to virtue knowledge, to knowledge self-control, to self-control perseverance, to perseverance godliness, to godliness brotherly kindness, and to brotherly kindness love. For if these things are yours and abound, you will be neither barren nor unfruitful in the knowledge of our Lord Jesus Christ."

Growing up in my childhood, I used to view virtue as glamour, riches, and honor. I have this painted picture in my mind of someone dressed in the finest clothing, head held high, calling themselves virtuous. Or the animated avatar of a boss who wears a tilted hat on her head, shaped with an hourglass figure, and high heels that pierces the floor. That was what I identified virtue as growing up. I always envision myself prosperous. I once *focused* on gaining riches, living in a huge home, and performing in front of multitudes. Keyword here is *focused*. But God revealed to me that virtue is not about gaining materialistic blessings. God gives us free will to dream big, to set high standards for ourselves, not for us to idolize it. He gives us abundance to enjoy. With abundance comes an authentically changed heart. God revealed to me that virtue is not about gaining materialistic blessings. Virtue is an authentic character achievement that leads you into obtaining the wealth you desire.

Virtue is sometimes mistaken as a materialistic gain instead of an inward maintenance. Unfortunately, there are people who struggle with believing that they are virtuous. There are some who struggle with believing that virtue is living within them because of the misunderstood mechanism of obtaining virtue. Of the many definitions of virtue, Merriam-Webster defined virtue as the conformity to a standard or right; a particular moral excellence. In other words, virtue is a characteristic. Not a materialistic value.

Virtue is obtained by maintaining a healthy spirit with the outcome of righteous morals. Virtue is not obtained by materialistic possession. It is an inward manifestation of God's exuberant wisdom and power. To develop the fruit of virtue, you must first check your heart. Are you mean-spirited and selfish? Or are you compassionate and insightful? Pray to develop a healthy heart; to love God with all of your heart, mind, and soul. As you learn to authentically love God's people, virtue will naturally flow through you. You begin to love what He loves and hate what He hates. You begin to develop Godly character. He opens your eyes to the unseen. Allow God to work on your character throughout your heart, mind, and soul. You will then notice virtue - moral excellence – developing within your identity.

The Virtuous Woman
One of my favorite biblical characters is the description of the Proverbs 31 woman.

"An excellent woman [one who is spiritual, capable, intelligent, and virtuous], who is he who can find her? Her value is more precious than jewels and her worth is far above rubies or pearls."
Proverbs 31:10 AMP

This woman is described as virtuous. Her character represents her love for not only her husband, but also her love for her household, her female servants, her community, and her love for God. This woman lives life to the best of her ability. She is confident in her identity as a woman with the determination to make an impact on others. She selflessly obtains knowledge so that she can provide solutions. "Many women are capable but you surpass them all!" (Verse 29). As a result, the people who watch her are amazed at what she does. She inspired other women to become the best version of themselves. Those who were in close proximity benefited from this woman. Who's to say that you're not capable of becoming a strong virtuous woman?

Not to forget the man reading this, don't limit yourself to what God can do within you. You are called to be a virtuous man of God. You have gifts within you that you can contribute to others. You're never alone. There's a dying need for more brothers in the body of Christ to rise up and put their hands to the plow. You may be the only man in your church with focused vision to fulfill God's purpose in your life. Think of the men who are struggling to maintain their household. Think of the men who are struggling with fear. Think of the man who is suicidal. It you haven't grasped an understanding of your purpose, think of your struggles and weaknesses. God called you out of darkness and into His marvelous light so that you can impact others for the benefit of His kingdom. You most definitely have a place in this world to be a light vessel. It could be as simple as showing up to work to demonstrate an example of how to live a godly lifestyle in moral excellence. Because you are Christian, there are people watching you to find God within you.

Remember, virtue is an inward manifestation of God's exuberant wisdom and power. It is a characteristic living within your DNA that is meant to be carried out in your lifespan. It is a beneficial part of your identity. Are you willing to become all that God has predestined you to become, to make a remarkable impact in your household and community?

I...Am Heard

Develop Your Roar!

Isaiah 52:7 NKJV

How beautiful upon the mountains Are the feet of him who brings good news, who proclaims peace, Who brings glad tidings of good things, Who proclaims salvation, Who says to Zion, "Your God reigns!"

Speak up, oh, daughter! Speak up, oh, son! Someone is awaiting to hear your story. There's someone who is voiceless, looking for ways to make their voice heard. You just so happen to be one of the many seeds planted within their lives to bring the best out of them.

It can become so easy to feel outweighed when others around you are speaking louder than you. We have many different sectors of influence, where creatives with many different skills are prospering in their purpose. But then there are others who are just getting started. Can I give you some encouragement? In the darkest moments where you feel as though you're unheard, that is when your soul speaks the loudest. You just have to build the confidence to use your voice to speak as loud as your soul.

I was watching the latest version of The Lion King - one of my favorite childhood movies. One of the scenes that stood out to me the most was when Simba and his father – Musafa – spent a moment together during sunrise one morning. They both reclined upon the highest rock of their kingdom. Musafa told Simba in these exact words, "Look Simba. Everything the light touches is our kingdom. A king's time as ruler rises and falls like the sun. One day Simba, the sun will set on my time here, and will rise with you as the new king." Simba was enthused to know that he would be king one day. He told everyone that he saw, he sang about it and even prepared himself for kingship. What he didn't know was that he had an enemy on his side setting him up for failure - his Uncle Scar.

I wanted to jump into the movie to let Simba know that it's not wise to let everyone know your future. I wanted to tell him to discern his enemies! I know the feeling of being set up for failure due to my big mouth telling everyone God's secrets for my future. It's unfortunate to discover that the very ones who are closest to you can sometimes be your haters! They can be the very ones seeking to limit your roar!

Little Simba wore his identity as king at a young age. He took risks. He was fearless. Most of all, he constantly practiced building the biggest threats to his enemies – his roar. Anytime a lion roars, all of the animals of the kingdom knows that the king has stepped on scene. The animals that are prey to the lion make no hesitations to linger. They duck for cover quickly. Simba may not have possessed a life-threating roar to his enemies, but he was confident in his identity at a young age. He knew that if he kept practicing, the animals in the kingdom would eventually take him seriously.

There came the point in the movie where Simba was set up by Scar's plot to create chaos in the kingdom. There was a hoard of animals surging in a dangerous valley where Simba needed rescuing. Simba's father was called to save him, which placed his father in jeopardy. While Simba was rescued, his father was fighting for his life on a cliff. Scar didn't bother rescuing Musafa. Instead, he purposely scratched his paws intending to kill him. Simba saw his father fall off of the cliff into a world of death, not realizing that Scar was the one who caused the death. Simba was heartbroken, thinking that his need of rescuing was the cause of his father's death. After watching his father's death, Simba felt diminished and highly incapable of taking his position as king. Scar instilled fear into Simba, driving him to travel far away into a foreign land until he was ready to come back home.

Fast forward to Simba's call to be king had come into full effect. As previously mentioned, Simba had lost his confidence when his father died. He spent a long period of time in a foreign land. He then awakened to his calling as king once he found out that his homeland was in trouble. He had to stand up and battle in one of the most life-threatening fights of his life. His Uncle Scar revealed himself as an enemy, even admitting that he killed Simba's father. Mmmm. Isn't that heartbreaking? This was the real breaking point that ignited the passion in Simba to ROAR! To take a stand and fight for his legacy as the king of his territory!

I mention this entire story to encourage you to fight for your legacy. There is a greater future that withholds the fulfillment of God's plans. He wants to reveal Himself as the Great I Am through your life. No matter where you are in the journey towards your destiny, roar like you have authority over every area of your life. Roar! Speak up! Intercede for your family. Fight for your legacy. Live in your identity. Roar over every principality and all forces of darkness! Roar over every emotional thought in your mind that is against the standards of Christ.

Your roar is your gifts and talents. If you are a writer, your roar is in every written word that you publish. If you are a singer, your roar is in the harmonies of your diaphragm. If you are a dancer, your roar is in every position as you leap across the floor. If you are a speaker, your roar is in the depth of every life-giving word that rolls off of the tip of your tongue. If you are a poet, your roar is in the rhythmic tone within the spoken word of your art. Whichever talent that God has gifted you with, you have to come to a place of self-discovery where you allow your roar to be heard louder and louder each time you are faced with the opportunity to lead someone else to become a better version of themselves. God has gifted you with something unique to reveal His existence within you.

> You were created with an identity.
> Within your identity, your soul seeks to speak.
> So, when you speak,
> Don't just speak to be heard.
> Speak to ROAR.

Arnesjah Miller

I...Am Victorious
Overcoming the World by Faith

1 John 5:4 NKJV

"For everyone born of God is victorious and overcomes the world; and this is the victory that has conquered and overcome the world—our [continuing, persistent] faith [in Jesus the Son of God]."

The deadly words that we speak over ourselves can diminish our authority to overcome life's obstacles. This calls for a perspective shift. I completely understand what it is like to doubt positive outcomes when faced with detrimental situations. I know what it's like to feel defeated after expecting to win. I've experienced the mental weight of feeling useless after being told that I'm unqualified for a job position. Can I give you some encouragement? Your faith in God is what makes you victorious.

The measure of your faith is what will produce the measured results of your expected outcome. Like pouring 5 ounces of water in a glass cup, you are going to expect to drink 5 ounces of water. There's no expansion nor disappearance of the water. This is obvious to the human eye. But what will require faith is if you just so happen to be extremely thirsty and all you have is 5 ounces of water. If 5 ounces of water doesn't usually quench your thirst, it would be your great faith in God with the expectation that the 5 ounces of water will sustain you for the time being.

Now, what makes you victorious and overcome the world by your faith in Jesus Christ is when you are faced with an uncontrollable interruption. There was an unforgettable moment in my life where God gave me the victory in the face of the enemy. During a particular season in my life where I was living with my dad, he was also married to a woman who happened to be abusive towards me for quite a few years. She'd always manipulate me to trigger a fight.

One morning, while I was listening to worship music and practicing poetry, she decided to flicker with the electricity box in our home to turn the music off in my room. I had enough of her manipulating with me. So, I decided to defend myself by approaching the problem. To be honest, I did not approach the problem in a cordial manner, which unfortunately resulted in her fighting me. This fight was the worst fight that her and I ever had. It was to the point where I ended up with bruises and the cops were involved.

She intensified the situation by causing me to look like the abuser. I was then faced with a restraining order where I was forced to move out of my dad's house for a few weeks. Thankfully, I had just rededicated my life to the Lord a few weeks before, so I knew to trust in God during my circumstance. He then provided friends and family members to support me. Was I angry? Heck yes! I was hurt. I was mad at the fact that my dad was seemingly under some curse but not doing his best to fight for me. Did I seek revenge? No. Causing another fight would cause even more problems. All I had to do was pray and put my faith in God. I had actually gone to the courthouse to prove document all of the times throughout the years she abused me.

Fast forward to the day both she and I attended court. Though I was nervous, something within me told me that I had already won the trial. I a feeling that I would live with my dad again. Long story short, the woman revealed her true colors in the courtroom and the judge pieced together who was truly innocent and who was not. Thanks be to God I won the case and was able to live with my dad again. Since that very day, I haven't seen her. Prayerfully she's in a better place and state of mind.

My circumstance was evidence that I am victorious and I overcome the world by my faith in Jesus Christ. I didn't have to do much. When I was restrained against my dad's home, all I had to do was pray. When I needed help, God sent a provision. When I needed God to fight my battles, I just had to answer the judge's questions and allow God to take care of the enemy. It was because I stepped out of the way to allow God to take over, I received the victory.

This same victory is available for you as well, beloved. God has given you the victory over your circumstance. The way to access this victory is to change your perspective of how you intend to overcome the battle. Pray, fast, and worship through the trial. Be still and know that God is The Great I Am. Stand aside and watch God use you to reveal His victory. It's all in the measure of your faith. Will you trust Him?

I…Am Creative

Benefiting Others with Your Creativity

Genesis 1:27 NKJV

"So God created man in His own image; in the image of God He created him; male and female He created them."

As Creatives, we have the tendency to feel as though we are out of this world. We see things differently in life. We stand firm on our opinion. We get frustrated when we are constricted to man's regulations. We desire to work outside the box. We enjoy our personal space and to feel comfortable being alone. We delight in art. We develop inspiration instantly. Often times we create from the sensitivity of our emotions. We feel another person's pain and can paint a picture about it. We have abnormal tendencies. We have a respect for nature. As Creatives, we are aesthetically inclined to God's messages, which is why it is important that we know our identity as God's creation.

God created us in his image so that we may carry out his will. He created us with the intention of making this world a better place. Before the earth was completely formed, God saw that darkness was within the face of the deep. God saw that there needed to be a separation between dark and light. So, He divided the light from darkness. I believe that in order for this world to become a better place, God is using His creation to display His phenomenal existence. God saw that in order for this world to know who He is, He would have to make the earth suitable for mankind to dwell.

Our Master created the lights in the universe, the streams of waters, the vegetation from the ground, and the animals of the land just for us to have dominion over the earth. God gave us the mission to live in His image so that we too may be creative just as He. With all of the infinite power that God contains, we can never become God Himself. But we are given permission to represent Him, to conform into His likeness for the benefit of His kingdom.

What some people haven't accepted is their identity as a creative. You know how it goes when mom and dad tell their son or daughter that they need a real education in order to succeed in life. So, the child goes to college to earn a degree that they may not use in the future. Deep within, they know that they have a love for art. They go to make ways to present their art as a hobby. Yet, because of the hardship and pressure that comes with making a living, they just treat their artwork as a hobby instead of a lifestyle.

Though education and skill are highly important in life, it is an even greater benefit to utilize your God-given gifts that are already instilled within your identity. It is important to not allow your gifts to go to waste. Your creative instinct is what God has instilled within you since birth. Just as God told Jeremiah, "Before I formed you in the womb I knew you; before you were born I sanctified you; I ordained you a prophet to the nations (Jeremiah 1:5)." God had already instilled within Jeremiah's identity who he would become and what he would fulfill in the earth during that time. You may have a passion to create music, write books, help people through your multi-talented skills. Whatever God has purposed you to fulfill, seek God's plans and trust Him in your pursuit. Don't hang onto the opinions of others. There are some people in your life who have gone as far as they want to go with their dreams. There are others in your life who have given up due to fear. However, beloved, other people's purpose is not your responsibility to carry. God has given you the responsibility to plant seeds that will help them to pursue their purpose.

When you are a distinct creative, you have a challenging task that requires you to build something great from your imagination. Some people think your creativity is worthless. However, God sees your creativity as greatness. The more you spend time nurturing, building, and applying knowledge to your craft, you begin to see it manifest into a meticulous masterpiece beyond your imagination.

Now, I want you to realize something special about God's gift to you. If God created every natural source from the soil of the earth, how much more creativity will God pull from your creative instinct? And if God revealed Himself through Jesus to show us the way, granting us the ability to do even greater works than Himself, then what are you holding back from? Why are you limiting yourself from becoming all of what The Great I Am has predestined you to become?

As a result, utilizing your creative ability benefits the rest of humanity. Creatives have the power to display art in a form that grants inspiration to the downtrodden. Do you have the power to influence? You contain the aesthetic enthusiasm to bring light into a room full of darkness. There are others who aren't as creative as you who are looking to make the best out of life. So, go ahead, my love. Share with the world the creation that God has birth within you.

I…Am NOT Suicidal
Combating the Voices in Your Mind

John 10:10 KJV

The thief cometh not, but for to steal, and to kill, and to destroy: I am come that they might have life, and that they might have it more abundantly.

There are voices in our head that seemingly overpower the voice of God. These voices of deception are aimed to take you out. You may wonder why you have to go through the challenges that you face - challenges that are worse than you could ever imagine. You may every-now-and-then think about committing suicide. But committing suicide is not God's will for you, and you know this. So, you may wonder, why do these thoughts appear?

Suicidal thoughts are derived from one particular root that has sprouted from many seeds. These seeds could consist of rejection, fear, depression, insecurity, abandonment, and loneliness. With any of these emotions lingering within your soul, suicidal thoughts can easily form when you're faced with a situation that appears to be impossible to overcome.

I've had my share of overwhelming suicidal thoughts. In attempt to prevent them from defeating my life, each time a suicidal thought comes to mind I push myself out of my emotions to remind myself of God's plans and promises for me. It seems easier said than done. It truly takes effort to acknowledge the weight of oppression and renounce every thought that it sends. I no longer allow suicidal thoughts to play with my future. I'd be oppressed with spiritual suicide. I'd literally rebel and tell God that I'm not going to do what He's commanded me to do. I've pondered on plots to run away from my calling, to get away from the spiritual warfare that comes with it. I believed the lie that nobody really cares about the work that I produce. I even looked for validation through the opinion of man. Through it all, I came to realize that my calling is not created by man. God is the author and finisher of my faith, and if He calls me to a specific purpose, then He's got my back.

You see, Satan seeks to sever your confidence. He knows that greatness shines through you. He knows that you are capable of bringing souls out of darkness and into the marvelous light of God. He doesn't want the truth to come from out of you. But instead of backing down you must fight.

Fight back by speaking the word of God over yourself every day. Meditate on scripture relating to your identity as well as God's love for you. Treat God's word as if it is your daily supply of vitamins for your soul. You need this word in order to survive in this world. At the end of the day, battles don't last always.

God has birth wisdom within you. You are an exhibit of creative ideas, strategy, and stories that can benefit others. Your personality, your presence, the way that you love people is heaven's home for the lost souls. Hence, it is not God's thoughts that are attempting to take you out. When tormenting thoughts come to mind, renounce them aloud. Stand your ground fearlessly. Cast down every thought and imagination that exalts itself against the knowledge of God, and bring every thought to the obedience of Christ as Second Corinthians 10:5 encourages.

Jesus loves you. He is leading you each and every day towards the abundance of life that is in store for you. This abundance is not mistaken for only material blessings. This abundance also has to do with the maturity and wealth that God created you to be calm. You are abundant! And there is nothing that suicide can do to try to take you out.

Suicidal thoughts are stemmed from the roots of fear, oppression, offense, and death. There is divine power in the words you speak. If you are battling with suicidal thoughts, pray this prayer with me:

Lord, I repent for allowing offense to control me. I cast my cares upon you (1Pet. 5:7)

I repent for any self-ambition, self-will, or anger towards your will for my life (Phi. 2:3-4).

Oppression, be far from me, for I am established in righteousness (Is. 54:14)

I rebuke and cast out every tormenting thought that would attempt to oppress me.

I break the bonds of death, attempted death, and the fear of death, and I command them to leave and never return, in the name of Jesus.

I am perfected in God's love, for perfect love casts out fear (1Jn. 4:18)

I loosen the grips and strongholds of fear that would attempt to forfeit my future.

I rebuke and cast out all spirits of anger, rage, and offense that would attempt to oppress my mind (Ec. 7:7).

I rebuke and cast out doublemindedness, suicidal thoughts, and isolation, in the name of Jesus (James 1:8).

Deliver me from my oppressors.

Deliver me from fear of man, fear of failure, fear of poverty, fear of rejection, fear of loss relationships, fear of broken relationships, fear of marriage, fear of success, and every fear that would attempt to abort my destiny.

I receive the spirit of love, power, and a sound mind (2 Tim. 1:7).

I ultimately command fear, oppression, offense, and death to leave and never return. In Jesus' name, Amen.

I…Am Innovative
4 Principles to Thrive as an Innovative

Genesis 1:31 NLT

Then God looked over all he had made, and he saw that it was very good! And evening passed and morning came, marking the sixth day.

Innovative (adj.)

tending to introduce something new or different.

If you contain any amount of creativity, you are indeed innovative. Do you have the ability to create or introduce something completely new and different? There's something about you that says, "I am different." This is amazing! Because often we see repeats of ideas but in different subjects in life. The only problem that I have noticed with innovators sometimes is that we find ourselves stuck all the while looking for the motivation to move forward. It can be quite challenging to see the bigger vision or attain the idea, yet lack the steps to build it up.

Another challenge that you may face is the lack of support. Your friends and family members may not sow into your vision. So then, you're really faced with the pressure to start from the ground up. Lastly, one of the worst hindrances you may face as an innovator is the spiritual battle with consistency in pushing forward with your extraordinary idea. Creating something that doesn't spark people's interest is not an easy take. Especially if it doesn't spark their bank account in return. Let's be honest. The beginning stages of innovating a new idea can be frustrating because of the lack of results that you are receiving. However, there is a solution that you must stick with if you want to see your vision come to pass. I've discovered the 4 principles for you to thrive as an innovative:

4 Principles to Thrive as an Innovative

1. Apply Prayer Towards Your Invention

The first and important principle that will help you to thrive as an innovative is to Apply Prayer Towards Your Invention. If God has given you an idea, what better way to flourish in it than in the supernatural realm of prayer? Prayer is where you will hear from God on behalf of strategies. The strategies that God give you will provide solutions, release dates, vision for the present and future time, answers to questions, and extraordinary trends.

Communication with God is your main source that will help you and your idea to expand beyond normality.

2. Remain Consistent with Your Daily Goals

The second principle that will help you thrive as an innovative is to Remain Consistent with Your Daily Goals. My definition of consistency is repetitious commitment towards a positive outcome. When you are consistent with your daily goals - I'm talking meeting the deadlines that you planned for yourself, committing to a simple task - you and your idea will benefit from it. Consistency makes you reliable. It helps you to be trustworthy towards your clients and the followers of your brand. I challenge you to make a daily commitment to be consistent with one important task. This could be writing a chapter a day for your next book. Contacting potential clients for your business. Creating an eBook each day. Exercising at the gym. Applying biblical meditation for twenty minutes to an hour. Once you feel you are ready to commit to another task add it to your to-do list.

As an author, I am always developing new ideas for books. When God gives me loads of information, I write it down immediately. Even if He wakes me up in the middle of the night. I write it down. Why? Because God is speaking. God is downloading beneficial words of encouragement, vision for graphics, and strategies to enhance the vision of my book. It is necessary to consistently write daily so that all of what God is pouring into me doesn't go to waste. God is a moving God. He doesn't waste any time. Neither should you.

3. Have Faith in Every Circumstance

The third principle that will help you thrive as an innovative is to Have Faith in Every Circumstance. I kid you not, as an innovative you are going to face uncomfortable roadblocks where you will have to figure out how to manage through it. There are times where you will question God's presence among you. You are literally starting from the bottom of the map and you are working your way up to the top. Success is not achieved overnight.

When you run into a problem where your finances have suddenly taken a toll, use wisdom and have faith that God will restore more than you could imagine in the future. When you are not receiving the results to draw people into your business, utilize resources for building clientele and have faith that God will give you insight for drawing in multitudes. Even more so, while you are in prayer, affirm the vision. Write down what God has shown you and then speak it in prayer. There's something about speaking aloud that generates your faith. That is why I always encourage to speak affirmations. In all that you do, seek to bring God the glory and benefit His kingdom.

4. Attain Confidence Within Yourself

The last beneficial principle that will help you thrive as an innovative is to Attain Confidence Within Yourself. You can apply all of the principles above - prayer, consistency, and faith - but if you lack confidence, these principles will be useless. God created you to be innovative so that you can confidently produce new things into the earth. Without confidence, you are burning valuable energy and wasting precious time. A lack of confidence will cause you to create ideas and then allow them to collect dust. It's like writing books just to hoard a room that no one will walk into.

Confidence is the key that will unlock doors for you. Once people see your hard work and notice your confidence within your presentation, they will believe in what you are producing. Confidence is how you make profit. Confidence will enhance your development. It will bring you more ideas. It will create many doors of opportunities. And it will manifest everything that you've been praying for. There you have it, my friend. If you take anything from this message, utilize the 4 Principles to Thrive As An Innovative and watch the bounty of good results flow in your life.

I…Am Favored

(Part 1)
The Calling of a Favored Innovator

Genesis 6:8 ESV
"But Noah found favor in the eyes of the Lord."

God had specifically created Noah to be an innovator of his time. Noah walked with God. Noah was a favored outsider. He did not participate with any of the corruption within his community. There was something peculiar about Noah, and no one noticed his indifference until God called him to make a difference in the world. God called Noah to build an ark - an extraordinary God-given invention that no one has ever heard of. No one else was given this idea or an idea of this kind because they didn't have enough faith to obtain favor with God. Can you relate to Noah? You know that you stand out from others, yet suddenly, God calls you to build or pursue something that is totally outside of the norm?

An innovator has a special grace to fulfill the works that he or she is called to. For Noah, he was graced to build an ark that was 300 cubits in length (450 feet in length), 50 cubits in width (75 feet in width), and 30 cubits in height (45 feet in height). Noah had the patience, the time, and the skill to build something that would make a major impact on the world.

When you are given the responsibility to create something that no one else was assigned to create, God will grace you to succeed in the assignment. This goes for anything you're purposed for. I've seen a mother of five children gracefully take care of her household with her husband. Not only is she a mother and a wife, she's also an owner of two big dogs. I've never seen her struggling to make it through life. Although I'm sure she has rough days, I admire how she manages her family well with a smile. God continues to favor her and her family because she is graced for the responsibility. I wouldn't expect myself to have five kids, own two dogs, and a be wife. Lord knows I'd lose my mind! I'm not even married yet! God is wise and well-knowing enough to not place those expectations on me because He knows the capacity that I can handle.

One of my responsibilities as an innovator is to manage Prayer Mats by Arnesjah, LLC. God has graced me to hand craft Prayer Mats out of t-shirts, leggings, and cami's. He's given me the patience to work on one Prayer Mat for seven to eleven hours. He's given me the idea to add beads, handmade pom-poms, and other accessories, and then sell the Mats to people. Selling Prayer Mats are not an easy responsibility. However, God has graced me to create them. It takes a great amount of prayer, consistency, faith, and confidence to carry out God's vision.

Carrying out the vision is very important. If you do not take the necessary steps that is freely open for you, you can cause yourself to be unprepared for the supernatural moves of God. I wonder what would have happened if Noah didn't finish building the ark while the flood swept over the earth. I believe that God is truly patient when it comes to caring out His vision. However, there comes a time when God gives you a stern call to produce the fruitful gift within you. If you do not make the necessary faith-moves when He calls you to complete an assignment, then how will you fulfill God's will? Now, don't think that moving by faith is all about moving urgently without God's plan.

Moving by faith is about moving out of willingness and obedience to God. You move when God lays a move deeply on your heart. It's like the weakened shaking in your spirit when God is calling you to the altar at church. It's the overwhelm of His presence that falls upon you when you receive a prophecy. It's the heated fire you feel in your soul when you're praying. It's even the silent whisper He speaks. It's the *knowing* in your soul – when you know that you know that you know! He speaks through signs and wonders as reminders that you're in His will. It's the confirmation through scripture that He leads you to. That is when God speaks to give you direction on what moves to make by faith. You just have to trust Him at His word. He will never lead you astray. EVER. With that being said, do not despise your small beginnings. The Lord is excited to see work begin (Zechariah 4:10).

I...Am Favored

(Part 2)
Obtaining Faith to Produce Favor

Genesis 18:3 NKJV

My Lord, if I have now found favor in Your sight, do not pass on by Your servant.

I...Am Chosen

How many times has God blessed you and you denied the blessing because you felt as though you did not deserve it? Or maybe you've waited for God to bless you with the one and only thing that you've waited years to receive, and now that it was time to receive it, you've doubted that it was a blessing sent from God.

I am reminded of when Abraham and Sarah were favored to be impregnated at such an old age. Abraham had a relationship with God where he was able to converse with God on a regular basis. At the age of 99, the Lord visited Abraham making a promise of what his future would hold. Abraham's future was promised to be not only fruitful, but he and Sarah would also bear a child within the next year.

Let's draw into Sarah's promise. Have you ever felt like Sarah? Barren, an outsider, a one-of-a-kind-soul, chosen, yet wondering if God truly loves you enough to fulfill his promise? I know I have! God told Abraham that Sarah would be a mother of nations. Sarah laughed because she thought it would be impossible at their age.

Isn't it interesting how God shows up when we least expect it? He shows up in the most seemingly unfavorable areas of our lives just to show how much of a miraculous God He is. He grants us favor in the most illogical ways, beyond our human understanding. That's what makes God Mighty. The human mind cannot fathom the meticulous appearances of God's nature. He shows himself strong when we are weak. He provides for us at the last minute when we run out of options. And I believe that God does this so that we, human beings, do not manipulate our desires within our own strength. Because if we make an impossible situation possible out of our own will, we cannot give the credit to God.

I've read some of my favorite stories in the Bible where I've realized that it was faith and favor upon God's chosen ones that granted them access to their promise. The peculiar people who were sensitive to God's movements were granted favor because of their faith in God. In addition to their faith, they asked God for favor and it was granted unto them. Let's briefly take a look at a few people who were granted favor due to their faith and relationship with God.

Abraham and Sarah's Favor (Genesis 18)
Three men brought confirmation of God's promise for Abraham and Sarah. Abraham asked for them to not pass him by if he had found *favor* with God.

Ruth's Favor from Boaz (Ruth 2)
Ruth had faith to leave her hometown to go work in an unknown land. Then receives favor in the sight of Boaz as she gleaned his field. Ruth's faithfulness granted her access to an unexpected blessing from Boaz. She asked Boas for a favor (Ruth 2:13) and she received her blessing to eat with the other servants. It was for bidden for Ruth to be amongst the people in Bethlehem because she was a Moabite, and unfavorable foreigner. Even though Ruth did not belong in the land, she was favored by God because of her faithfulness.

Noah's Favor with God (Genesis 6)
Noah found favor in the eyes of the Lord because of his faithful relationship with Him. Noah lived in a detrimental land. God was ready to wipe the earth, but God favored Noah because He knew that Noah was faithful. Noah was chosen to invent an ark that would preserve the future blessings of the Lord. God saw fit that Noah, his family, and the animals were the only good things to preserve in a decaying generation. This is an example of when you have favor with God, those who are in close proximity with you obtain a favor as well.

Job's Favor with God (Job 10:12)
Job says, "You have granted me life and favor, and Your care has preserved my spirit." I wonder how is it that Job believed that God granted him favor in the midst of an unfavorable circumstance. Job was already favored by God because there was no one like him in the earth. He was a blameless, upright man who feared God and shunned evil (Job 1:8). Job was stripped from all that he owned. He was ridiculed because of his poverty. Yet Job remained faithful to trust that God favored him. I believe that there was an extraneous measure of faith within Job for him to believe that God would restore all that he lost. Sure enough, through all of his sorrows, tests, questions, and misery,

God restored twice as much of what he had before **after he prayed for his friends**. Though his friends audaciously ridiculed him, he still prayed faithfully for them. This is a great revelation to know that no matter what others may do to you, through persistent faith, God can manifest the breakthrough that you've been waiting on.

Mary's Favor to Conceive Jesus

In Luke 1, the arch-angel, Gabriel, tells Mary that she is favored and blessed among women. There was no one like Mary, chosen to conceive our Lord and Savior of the world. This favor she obtained, she didn't have to ask for it. It was predestined for her to experience this miracle. Her faith as well as her relationship with God granted her favor to reproduce the Promised Messiah.

Now do you understand how God grants favor through faith? Favor is not obtained through someone magically casting favor upon your life. Favor is not obtained through utilizing crystals. Favor is not obtained through rituals. None of those mechanisms are of Christ. It is through your faith and your relationship with the Father that you are blessed to receive favorable miracles in the most unfavorable, uncommon circumstances. I feel led to lead you into prayer in this moment, to ask God for favor to be released upon your life. Including the grace to carry out the favor once He releases it upon you.

Set your heart in a position to receive the promises of God in this moment. This prophetic activation prayer will stretch your faith. So, you must believe that God can and will produce exceeding and abundant favor over your life. If God can release miracles over Abraham and Sarah, Ruth, Noah, Job, Mary, and other people in the Bible, believe that God is the same God that can release abundant favor upon your life. Are you ready to pray? Let's go!

Father, in Jesus' name, I thank You for choosing me as your favored one.

I thank you for predestining me to carry out Your will upon the earth (Romans 8:29-30).

I thank You for already establishing to give me more than what my mind can imagine (Ephesians 3:20).

I thank You for all of your promises that you have in store for me and my future (Jeremiah 29:11).

Lord, forgive me for doubting your faithfulness. Forgive me for any of the times that I've rebelled against Your commands. For it is through my obedience and my trust in You that You bless me (Proverbs 16:20).

I forgive those who have ridiculed Your promises. Give me wisdom of when I am allowed to share your promises with others. Help me to guard Your promises within my heart, to protect them from the Devourer (Proverbs 4:23).

Lord, Your promises are yes and amen (2 Corinthians 1:20).

You are not a God that you should lie. You are not man that you should change Your mind (Numbers 23:19).

Lord, the words that You speak quickens the spirit, they are life and truth (John 6:63).

So, I receive every promise that You have in store for me. Even if I have to preserve in waiting, it is by faith that I already receive Your unseen blessings (Romans 8:24-25).

By faith, I believe that I have found favor and high esteem in Your sight and with man. I will trust in You with all of my heart, and lean not unto my own understanding. In all of my ways, I acknowledge You and You shall direct my paths (Proverbs 3:4-6).

Lord, allow Your Word to be the lamp unto my feet and the light unto my path (Psalms 119:105).

Lord, bless me and keep me. Make your face shine upon me and be gracious unto me. Lord lift Your countenance upon me, and give me peace (Numbers 6:24-26).

I love You Lord. Thank You for favoring me.
I receive all of these things. In Jesus' name I pray, Amen.

What if your comfortability
was stolen from you
so that you can become comfortable
with who you were truly
created to be?

What if comfortability
is only the icing on the cake
of the layers
of all that it would take
to soar upon your destiny?

What if comfortability
was a passport of visitations,
temporary encounters
that appeared and vanished
as they pleased?

What if everything you've studied about God
became uncomfortable to bare?
Would you still pursue your purpose
to live in your God-identity?

I...Am Fearless
Rejecting Comfortability to Overcome Your Fears

2 Timothy 1:7 NKJV

For God has not given us a spirit of fear, but of power and of love and of a sound mind.

One of the best ways to overcome fear is to step outside of your comfort zone. All it takes is one step...out of your mind. It takes one step...to step into a discovery of the power that has lived within you all along. It takes one step...to look fear in the eyes and point out its non-existence. Fear is an ungodly capacity. It is a realm of captivity that has traveled throughout generations. It seeks to trap you in a cave with darkness' limitations. Even though you are saved, fear trips you into remaining enslaved. But the crazy trick about fear is this, it's all in your mind!

God has embedded fearlessness within your identity, beloved. He has not given you the spirit of fear and timidity. He's given you the Spirit of power, love, and a sound mind (self-control). You have the power to overpower fear. God has given you the Spirit of love - a perfect passion that casts out all fear (1 John 4:16). Let alone, God has given you the authority over your emotions - to have self-control.

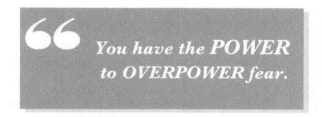

> **You have the POWER to OVERPOWER fear.**

Believe it or not, your emotions are what triggers fear to operate in your life. Emotions run rapidly; it changes within an instant. One moment you're experiencing a bliss of joy. Then next, you can become sadden. One moment you feel brave enough to pursue a challenge. Then when you think too far into details, you back away. It's okay, you're human. Think about a time when you were fearful of doing or saying something that you normally would not do. What thoughts do you think triggered you to say no to the very thing you were challenged to fulfill? Was it a speaking opportunity that you turned down because you believed the lie that nobody wants to hear what you have to say?

Was it a business idea that you turned down because you felt as if nobody wanted to buy your products or services? Was it your own identity that you've run away from because you're having a hard time believing in yourself? Well, in actuality, people won't know what you're offering unless you demonstrate your best. It just takes one step out of your mind. I promise you, there is someone dying for what you have to offer.

It is in those moments when you feel the limited thoughts in your mind preventing you from climbing hurdles and defeating demons. I've had my fair share of fear-battles. So, I came up with the strategy: 4 Mechanisms to Overcome Fear. Applying this strategy has helped me to overcome my fears:

4 Mechanisms to Overcome Fear

1. Recognize negative thinking.

Become more aware of negative thoughts. Some will find this mechanism easy and some will find it hard. Those who have lived with negative thinking majority of their life will find it harder to recognize the difference between their thoughts. This mechanism requires you to meditate on scripture daily to feed your mind, soul, and spirit with God's thoughts. Once you've recognized the thought, take it captive by submitting it to the Word of God.

2. Speak scripture-based affirmations of confidence, victory, and self-esteem...meditate on it DAILY.

You may battle with more than one spirit of affliction. Whether it be oppression, depression, low self-esteem, poverty, comparison, lust, greed, unbelief, the list goes on. Any spirit that is not compatible with power, love, and a sound mind is not of God. So, you must recognize these thought patterns and affirm the opposite (the truth) over yourself. A few examples of these affirmations are exactly what this book consist of:

I am beautifully and wonderfully made (Psalm 139:14).

I am confident, for Greater is He that is within me than He that's within the world (1 John 4:4).

I am healed, for God has restored me to health and healed my wounds (Jeremiah 30:17).

I am powerful, for God has given me the keys to the kingdom of heaven (Matthew 16:19).

I am more than a conqueror, no weapon formed against me shall prosper (Isaiah 54:17).

3. Challenge yourself to make bold moves outside of your comfort zone.

Use wisdom as you make these moves. Please do not go and approach people, places, and things with the wrong motives. Fear's goal is to cripple your effort to achieve greatness. So, your main goal in mind should be to make bold moves that will help you to gain the confidence to follow God's will faithfully. For instance, if you have a fear of speaking to strangers, compliment someone while you're in public. People love the feeling of being noticed. If you lack confidence in your evangelism or prophetic gifting, pray for God to lead you through vision of who to prophesy to in public. I've tried this plenty of times and God has never failed me. The key is to ask God for specific details and He will give you vision of the color of someone's outfit. He may even give you the first initial of their name. He will give you insight of what to tell them and share the testimony of the Lord. God is strategic and He delights in speaking to His people. Doing this will heighten your prophetic anointing and deeper revelation when in prayer.

4. Step out of your comfort zone to give a small token of kindness to your coworkers if you fear leading a group activity.

You'd be surprised how appreciative your coworkers will be when you show them recognition. I used to be timid of influencing my coworkers or sharing the gospel because for one, it was a corporate setting and we're limited to openly sharing our religious beliefs. Secondly, I was the youngest at my job! I'd think that my sophisticated coworkers would take me seriously. So, instead of cowering into fear, I stood up to the challenge to make an Empowerment Jar. I called it the UP jar which means *Unifying Peace in The Work Place*. This left me without a burden to approach my coworkers every day during our busy schedule. All they had to do was pull a note from the jar and allow God to speak into their life. I was surprised to see how excited my boss was to use it. I encourage you to step out of your comfort zone and give it a try. Let God use you in the workplace.

With the 4 Mechanisms to Overcome Fear, you will find yourself more confident, resilient, and fearless to live in your identity. You are fearless and wonderfully made, says the Lord. Receive it. Believe it. Embrace it.

I…Am Free

Loosened from Sin

John 8:31-36 NKJV

*"Then Jesus said to those Jews who believed Him, "If you abide in My word, you are My disciples indeed. And you shall know the truth, **and the truth shall make you free**." They answered Him, "We are Abraham's descendants, and have never been in bondage to anyone. How can You say, 'You will be made free'?" "Jesus answered them, "Most assuredly, I say to you, whoever commits sin is a slave of sin. And a slave does not abide in the house forever, but a son abides forever. Therefore, **if the Son makes you free, you shall be free indeed**."*

When you abide in Jesus, you are free from sin, forever. Sounds simple, huh? The challenge we face is carrying out these words given to us by Jesus. Our flesh is corrupt because we've grown accustomed to the comfortability of our environment. Like someone who has used drugs since adolescent, they've struggled to abstain from drug use because they are accustomed to using drugs. They've created a habit of gaining pleasure in an unhealthy way. Their body has to practice the discipline of abstaining from drugs in a step by step process in order to fully mature from drug-abstinence. It can be difficult to break unhealthy cycles, which is the same scenario occurs with sin.

Let me first address sin because there are some people who flinch at the word "sin" as if it's a disease. Sin is a highly uncomfortable word. It stings like a curse word to the world. But when in action, sin is unavoidable for many. As imperfect people, we sin quite often. The Bible states that if anyone hasn't sin, he is a liar. That is the truth. Just as if someone were to say they've never lied, they just told a lie and they've sinned.

Sin is not a habit that God condemns us for committing. However, He desires that we be not enslaved by it. God sent Jesus not to condemn the world, but to save the world (John 3:17). He came to lead us into life and life more abundantly (John 10:10). I believe that Jesus gives us life because He gives us a choice to either repent - turn from our filthy ways - and follow Him. Or, we can continue to live under the bondage of sin.

Although we know that sin is sin no matter how big or small, sin varies from different degrees in which we feel convicted upon. For instance, you can sin by lying to your boss to get a day off from work, or you can sin by having premarital sex. There are two different spectrums of sin where you may feel convicted. Which would you feel mostly convicted with? Lying to your boss to get a day off from work, or having premarital sex? You should feel convicted from both sins, but not everyone is in close relationship with God to feel convicted in both areas.

Relationship with God

Your relationship with God is just that - a relationship. When you received Jesus as your Lord and Savior, you've committed to communing a divine convent with Him as your King. Throughout scripture, it is stated that the church is the bride of Christ. Meaning, your relationship with God is a marriage, and He works daily to keep you Holy without spot, blemish, or wrinkle (Ephesians 5:27). He longs to keep your body whole until marriage, because He created sex to be a unified bond between on you and your purposed spouse. He knows the soul ties that are formed within sex. These soul ties create a spiritual connection of harmony where the two become divinely compatible within each other's likeness. Like when a woman conceives her baby, the embryo eventually forms into a fetus over time. The baby develops organs, muscles, bones, and expressions of its own identity, but carries the likeness in features of both mother and father. Within the mother's womb is a seed of harmony, love, and creation that both mother and father created through intimacy. It is the same scenario of the seed that is created when soul ties from.

During your singlehood season, God desires you to create a healthy intimate relationship with Him. This may sound strange to some, but when you grow deeper roots with the Lord, you begin to feel the nearness of God as if you're married to Him. You clothe yourself different. You desire purity. You value yourself at a greater measure. You honor God with your body. You turn away from self-destruction. You desire to obey God and follow His will for your life. Having an intimate relationship with God convicts you when you sin. It's your marriage with the Lord that reminds you of who you are. No one else and nothing else should get in the way of your relationship with the Lord. He fights for you constantly to be with Him. It is only by faith that you can receive His awe and wonder. If you are doubting God's existence, then sin won't feel as convicting, nor will you understand your marriage with Him. It is through reading the Bible that you will discover more of His love, compassion, mercy, grace, and freedom that is in Him. Your commitment with God is measured by your faith in Him. How far are you willing to journey with God? How big are you aiming to believe?

The subject of sin may feel a little uncomfortable for you. But I have to touch on areas of sin - in particular, premarital sex - that you may not be aware of. I haven't always had my relationship with God on point. I've learned from my sins so that I can show you the way to God through Christ Jesus. During my beginning phase of Christianity, I thought that it was okay to have premarital sex. On one end of the spectrum, I've heard that there was nothing wrong with it. On another end, I was told that it is unholy. At the time when I was in a relationship, I gave it a try because I thought it was okay. But boy did God convict me every single time! I became so convicted that I had to stop disobeying God's conviction. I told my fiancé at the time that God was calling me to a lifestyle of purity. Which meant we could no longer be intimate. No more hanging out in the hotel room. No more spending the night. It was a tough move to make, but I needed to be committed to my personal relationship with God. My level of conviction changed from the beginning of our dating season to our season of engagement.

You see, I have to express the raw truth that we've become accustomed to surface level Christianity where we think our Heavenly Father is passive about certain things such as premarital sex. I completely understand that you may struggle in this area. You feel the unescapable weight to pursue the urges. You think that if you were to just do it to get the feeling over with you'll feel fine. Even when you fall, you feel a heavy conviction afterward. It is a cycle of sin that is seemingly unbreakable in your life. Christ has already set you free from this sin. It's a matter of you activating your authority and discipline over the sin in that moment when temptation knocks at your door. There are some demons that are renounced by vocal declaration and affirmation, and there are some that require prayer and fasting.

And when He had come into the house, His disciples asked Him privately, "Why could we not cast it out?" So He said to them, "This kind can come out by nothing but prayer and fasting."
Mark 9:28-29 NKJV

When you fast and pray, be intentional about filling up your spirit with the Word of God. Eliminate all distractions. Cut off relationships that tempt you to remain in sin. Listen to your soul when you feel the temptation to sin. Write down scripture relating to purity, holiness, and discipline. Study scripture in the subject of transforming into the likeness of Christ. Dwell on God's love. Meditate on those scriptures daily. Tell God that you desire to honor Him with your body. Within all of these practices, you are training your mind, body, spirit, and soul to turn away from the sin-cycle.

Godly Conviction Levels

One woman may be a babe in Christ, learning the basics, and not fully committed to communing with God. She may not study scripture or meditate on the Word of God daily. She's still in discovery of her identity. Trying to figure out who God is and how to hear His voice. Hey, we've all been there, my friend. But within our relationship with God is growth. Not everyone grows on the same levels. You will look around you in the Christian community and notice that some have deeper convictions than others. By no means are we perfect. But for us who are chosen, we have a higher calling to greatness where we carry the holy glory of God, which engages us to carry the presence of God in every area of our lives. We have a greater measure of commitment where we must obey the heavy convictions of the Lord.

The Bible is not just stories and parables written in an ancient book. It is life-breeding oxygen for our spirit-man. It is truth derived from the Holy Spirit. It is the guidance that we need to our circulation of life. It is the mirror to our souls that helps us to discover God's original intent to create us in His likeness. As you read God's Word, you will find that His love for you helps you to overcome your battle with sin. You won't find freedom in God's Word if you lack the effort to meditate upon it and work it out by faith. Your daily commitment to growing in God's Word should ignite a fire in your soul. You will feel challenged. You will feel convicted at times. But there's nothing wrong with a little discipline. You will need it as you combat the darkness of this world. There are levels to this walk, my friend. Are you willing to commit to God for the sake of living freely in your identity?

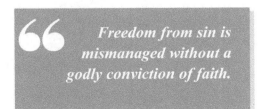

Freedom from sin is mismanaged without a godly conviction of faith.

Arnesjah Miller

I...Am Powerful

(Part 1)
Unlocking Your God-Given Power

Matthew 19:26 NKJV

But Jesus looked at them and said to them, "With men this is impossible, but with God all things are possible."

There is nothing that you cannot do. There is a magnificent God that lives on the inside of you. He is a joyous Friend that dances over you with joyful songs. He is a loving Father that loves you with all of His heart. He seeks to mold and sculpt you into His magnificent masterpiece. His plans for you are limitless. These aren't just flattering words. They are reminders of God's truth. Sometimes we hear the greatness of God and allow it to brush past our eardrums. Perhaps you woke up on the wrong side of the bed this morning. Maybe your day has been all out of wack. Hunny, this message is just what you need to snap back into your confident identity in Christ.

What makes you powerful is your confidence in your God-given rights. What makes you powerful is your metamorphosis into the likeness of Christ Jesus. What makes you powerful is accepting your identity as the offspring of the Living God. What makes you powerful is your inheritance within His Kingdom. What makes you powerful is applying the Word of God to your life. All of these great things that God created within you is to give you abundant life, and this abundant life exudes the power of God within you.

The Bible states in various scriptures of where our power resides:
> You are empowered with inner strength through God's Spirit as Christ makes His home in your heart (Ephesians 3:16).
> There is life and death in the power of the tongue (Proverbs 18:21).
> God strengthens you with His power when you are weak (Isaiah 40:29, 2 Corinthians 12:9).
> You can do even greater works than Jesus because of the Holy Spirit that resides within you (John14:12)
> The Lord gives you the power to obtain wealth (Deuteronomy 8:18)

It is by your level of faith that you have the ability to manifest this power. From your inner strength to the words that you speak out of your mouth, you have power. From your weakest moments to your greatest victories, you have power. By the works of the Holy Spirit, you have power. You have the power to produce wealth! Your prayers contain power.

I love the story of Hannah in the Bible. She was a woman who was barren for many years. She was married to Elkanah who also had a wife named

Peninnah. Peninnah had children while Hannah had none. She was still loved by her husband, but she was not okay with settling for nothing. She desired kids. She longed to have a family. She was sick and tired of being ridiculed by Peninnah who rubbed her barrenness in her face.

With all of the faith Hannah had within her, she made her way to the altar where Eli the priest reclined. With all of the heavy weight of agony and pain she withheld with her barren womb, her level of faith manifested her power in prayer. She had nothing but heartfelt passion, unspoken-of-hope, an unsurmountable desire to believe that God had more for her life than to live as a barren woman who was belittled by others. She knelt down on her knees and activated her power in prayer. This woman dug within the depth of her soul to reach the heart of God without any words coming out her mouth. Eli thought she was drunk. But she wasn't. It was her weeping faith that carried her powerful prayers to the heavenly heights of God's ear drums. Eli told her that her request had been granted. Sure enough, Hannah became pregnant with Samuel – who later on turned out to be one of the greatest leaders of Israel.

It was in the power of every area of Hannah's soul, every intricate part of her being that she manifested her blessing. She had faith in God first and foremost. She believed that God would answer her prayers. She then conceived the seed of her promise. There is something about when we get to our very last strand of hope that triggers the heart of God. There's something that moves heaven when we reach out far enough by faith to ask God for His blessing. There is something special about our connectivity to God to bring down resources from above.

God identifies you as powerful, beloved. Do you receive this power and will you apply it to your life? The Lord just gave me an image of someone who is reading this book that has come this far in the chapter and is still struggling his/her ability to receive the power of God. The powerful story of Hannah wasn't enough. You're say that there's something deeper that you're fighting with. You believe that you're always going to remain in the same position – weak, unstable, in lack, incapable, unqualified. You sometimes believe that the things you do are a waste of time. You believe in the lie that your prayers are powerless. You feel as though no one hears you. You have yet to make a difference in someone's life and you struggle to understand why God has chosen you to be a leader. Can I just encourage you, beloved? Let me just remind you plainly, change your mindset. You will never cross The Red Sea if you remain in Egypt. You will never cross the Jordan if you remain in the wilderness. You will never possess the land of Jericho if you never walk around the walls by faith. You will never defeat Goliath if you don't boldly face your giants. Come on now woman of God. Let's go man of God!

YOU ARE POWERFUL!

YOU ARE POWERFUL ENOUGH TO OVERCOME EVERY BARRIER! EVERY OBSTACLE!

EVERY GERNATIONAL CURSE!

EVERY NO!

YOU CARRY THE GLORY OF GOD!

Sometimes we need someone to reaffirm the greatness within us. We don't always see ourselves the way that God views us. I speak of the power of blessings that flows when we change our mindset and begin to speak life in the chapter entitled "I...Am Blessed". There comes a time when you have to decide to receive your God-given power from within and activate that thing. This God-given power unlocks doors to opportunities. This God-given power heals, delivers, and sets captives free. This God-given power is the Holy Spirit that reaches into the depth of one's soul and speaks of the unknown. There is no other path of life that I've found that has such power all obtained in one. That is why I am always going to stand firm on Christianity. We serve a dope God!

The only way to consistently activate the power of God within you is to practice utilizing it every day. You have to take your spiritual life seriously if you want to soar. So, I challenge you practice activating the power of God in the following areas:

1.   **Your Prayer Life** – There are two ways to do this.
    o   One way is to ask God to reveal to you an assignment that He specifically wants you to complete. Write it down. Fulfill the assignment. Ask Him for another assignment and carry it out. This activates the power of your faith to hear from God.

o   The second way is to ask God to lead you to pray for a friend. Genuinely pray for them. God may give you a specific area of their life to pray over. Send your friend a message letting you know that you're praying for them on that area. This activates the power of your faith to hear from God.

o   If you ever want to confirm what you've heard in your spirit is from God, ask God to give you scripture relating to the prophetic word. You can also ask the spirit if Jesus Christ came in the flesh. You should immediately hear a response within your spirit saying *yes*.

2.   **Biblical Meditation** – Practice meditating on one scripture every day. Find scripture that combats your negative thinking and bad habits. Utilize your journal or buy notecards to carry the scripture with you throughout the day. Memorize the scripture in the morning so that you can repeat it throughout the day. This activates your power to combat the enemy.

3.   **Areas of Fear** – I've discovered that fear is what limits power, love, and a sound mind from manifesting within you. So, do something you've never done before. Go for an adventure that you've always wanted to do but have always been afraid of doing. You know what you've told yourself you cannot do. Reverse every negative thought into a victorious godly thought. Believe it or not, this task expands your faith capacity and activates your power pursue greater things.

Arnesjah Miller

I...Am Powerful
(Part 2)
Move Your Mountain

Matthew 17:20-21 NKJV

So, Jesus said to them, "Because of your unbelief; for assuredly, I say to you, if you have faith as a mustard seed, you will say to this mountain, 'Move from here to there,' and it will move; and nothing will be impossible for you. However, this kind does not go out except by prayer and fasting."

When Jesus mentioned, "This kind does not go out except by prayer and fasting," He was talking about His disciples' inability to believe. Now, we see that Jesus was referring to the spirit that needed to be cast out of the demoniac in verses 14 to 16. However, His disciples lacked faith. They needed the power that comes with prayer and fasting to cast the demon out. There are instances where prayer and fasting are needed in order for certain demonic spirits to be cast out. However, faith is ultimately needed so that prayer and fasting can move [spiritual] mountains.

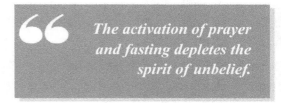

The activation of prayer and fasting depletes the spirit of unbelief.

In the midst of fasting and prayer, you are capable of moving mountains. When you have faith in God's power, you ignite the movement within the mountain in your life. For instance, a lack a self-control in one area of your life can cause you to become vulnerable to sin. Self-Control is the highest level of spiritual and mental achievement that you can amount to. Succeeding in self-control indicates that you are capable of overcoming mental strongholds, or what I call Mental Mountains.

For instance, let's say that you struggle with an addictive spirit that makes you vulnerable to gluttony. One of the several ways that you can overcome gluttony is by igniting your faith, believing in your heart that you have the power to overcome. With your level of faith, you're taking control over your body by the power of belief that you contain within your mind. This ignites your God-given power to declare authority over the mental mountain of gluttony. To fulfill this power, you will need to activate the principle of prayer and fasting so that the mountain ceases to have authority over you.

You are powerful when you are free from bad habits. You become powerless when such sins rule over your body, mind, and soul. God has designed you with an identity that authorizes you to obtain strength, confidence, discipline, and ultimately great faith. Your identity is the core of your being, awaiting to reach its highest potential. It is all of who you are. You are full of POWER!

You have authority over the adversary that threatens your destiny. You are wiser than the opinions of people that suppress your faith. You are skilled, talented, and flexible. You can move mental mountains by your confident trust and reliance in God. You are strongly committed to prayer and fasting because you are not a slave to your flesh. The atmosphere around you changes when you walk into the room, for you carry the glory of the Lord.

Lack of Faith = Lack of Power

Jesus' disciples could not cast the demon out of the man because just as Jesus stated, they *lacked faith* – trust and confidence in the power of God. **You cannot obtain the power of God if you don't believe in the power of God. Power is not just given you. Nor can power be given to you by any human being. Power is developed by your faith in God.** Wherever your flesh is ruling authority over your spirit, you are lacking faith in your God-given power. Let's dive a little deeper into this statement. I'm a witness to instances where some of the people within our Christian community have been ruled by the demonic oppression to sin. I'm talking fornication in ministry! Believing that it is okay! Let me tell you, when your emotional appetite of lust controls your sustainability of holiness, you've lost power the area of self-control. You can ruffle the leaves upon your tree, but there comes a time where people with power will get close to you to realize that you not only have rotten fruit, but you also lack authority over your mountain of lust.

I've witnessed manifestations of lust demons within ministry and I'm telling you, it ain't pretty to watch. There comes a point and time where a season of prayer and fasting comes upon a church house and suddenly, demonic spirits are exposed. This exposure is not intended to embarrass anybody. It is to reveal what needs to be dealt with in order to clean house. It is up to the person's activation of faith to take authority over his/her emotional habit. The sin(s) that you battle with are your emotions fighting against the power of your faith. Your emotions can be a mixture of sorrow, joy, anger, greed, or fear all within various moments.

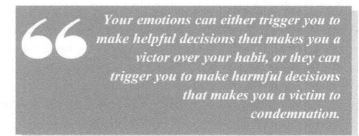

> *Your emotions can either trigger you to make helpful decisions that makes you a victor over your habit, or they can trigger you to make harmful decisions that makes you a victim to condemnation.*

When you get into the habit of constantly yielding to harmful decisions, your faith becomes crippled, making you powerless over your sin. You begin to feel defeated. You sometimes feel worthless to God. You tend to think negatively about yourself because you've sinned. You think God has ran away from you. You believe in the lie that you were meant to live with the sin forever. All of these waves of emotions paralyze your faith, making you powerless over the mountain of sin that God has *already* given you the power to move.

I've had plenty of moments where I'd backslide into an old sin. I'd feel a heaviness of doubt, fear, and separation from God. At the time, I lacked understanding of God's forgiveness and astounding love that covers a multitude of sins. Now that I have understanding, I stand on my faith that makes me whole.

You have to believe that you are strong enough to overcome every stronghold. Satan doesn't want you to believe that you are powerful than the kingdom of darkness. He doesn't want you to live freely within your identity because he wants to control your life. It's time to form new habits to get your mindset acclimated with your faith in God.

What is your reason to acclimate your faith in God? Everyone who is close to me knows that one of the biggest struggles of my life was my addiction to smoking marijuana. It's now my testimony which I talk in depth about in my first published book, Transparent Treasure: My Darkness Turned into Light.

My addiction to marijuana was controlling my life at one point. I longed for it. I bought too much of it. I had to have a puff of it throughout the day. There was a spirit influencing me to believe all of my troubles would pass away when I smoked. Some of my friends, at the time, even told me that there was nothing wrong with smoking weed. I was living in the illusion of gaining attention from guys. I was a wreck. But I eventually came to my breaking point.

My high was no longer pleasant, it became my depressant. I depended on marijuana to "hear from God". Not knowing that it wasn't the weed causing me to hear from God. Now that I think about it, God was with me all along, preventing me from smoking at times. I became uncomfortable every time I smoked. Believe it or not, I'd feel death surrounding me. I'd experience demonic encounters. My body became numb. Literally to the point where I couldn't feel anything while I was high. It scared me. I came to realize that God was calling me out of my addiction. He wanted to deliver me, to show me that the life that He has to offer is greater than the lifestyle of sin that I was dying in. God had other plans. He knew that the powerful woman that I was destined to become was the reason why I needed to acclimate my faith in God.

I've always knew that God had greater for me, but it was hard for me to believe because of my lack of popularity. I hated feeling unqualified. To be honest, I wanted nothing to do with Christianity during a long period of time at one point in my life because it always felt as if God wanted me to be less than who I knew I was to become. I hated feeling suppressed by rules and regulations. I didn't want God controlling my life, preventing me from living wild and free. But little did I know that being with God was the best and safest place that I could ever be. He knows my identity. He predestined me to be conformed into the likeness of Jesus Christ (Romans 8:29).

Had I remained dead within my addiction, I would have never experienced God's faithfulness. It was time to elevate above my circumstances. To arise above every shadow of death. My faith had to arise, to no longer compromise with the darkness of this world. No one else can live out my purpose for me. As much as I wish faith was transferable like money transactions, faith is not given to anyone. Faith is developed through relationship with God.

So, my questions for you is the same question that I had to face when it was time to move my mountain of addiction. What is your reason to acclimate your faith in God? Why do you believe it is necessary to grow your faith? What will you do to obtain the power of God to move your mental mountains? How long will you fester in fear? Fear is what keeps you bound to your lack of faith in God. Fear is what contaminates your mind and hinders you from believing in your prayers. Fear causes you to feel as though you are incapable of casting out demons. Fear convinces you to believe that you are *powerless*, beloved. We both know that 2 Timothy 1:7 tells us that God has not given you the spirit of fear and timidity, but of power, love, and a sound mind.

Jesus said, "If you have faith as small as a mustard seed, you *will* [be empowered and brave enough to] say to this *mountain* [addiction, fear of man, inferiority, incapability, etc.], 'Move from here to there,' and it will move; and nothing will be impossible for you,' (Matthew 17:20, emphasis added). Jesus was stating that you are well-qualified to move your mental mountains. It's not a physical mountain, but a spiritual mountain. You may be wondering how to move mountainous obstacles in your life. Perhaps your facing rejection, brokenness, bad habits, or unhealthy relationships. God has given you power and authority through prayer and fasting to move every mountain in your spirit.

I love what Jesus says in verse 21 of Matthew 17, "This kind does not go out except by prayer and fasting." You know those mental mountains you've been battling? They are overcome by prayer and fasting! Your prayer life needs to be on fleek as you acclimate in faith. Your fasting game needs to level up to as you discipline your flesh. The feeling of overcoming a mental mountain is rewarding! I kid you not! Deliverance is freedom. You feel accomplished, ready to take on the next level of your life.

Enhanced Supernatural Power
Another beautiful result of prayer and fasting is that your God-given power is enhanced. You become spiritually sensitive to the supernatural. Believe me, every time I pray and fast, it's like God speaks directly to me like an open book. I don't only just pray and fast. I take out the time, at least one hour or more in the middle of my day to worship and read the Bible. I get out of the

house for fresh air. I sometimes randomly have good and bad encounters with people. There's something about prayer and fasting that connects you closer to God. When you implement prayer and fasting into your life on a consistent basis, you will experience the results that Jesus talks about in Matthew 17:20-21. When you walk in acclimated faith, you begin to see demons flee. I've witnessed these results within my own life.

I encourage you to implement prayer and fasting to your lifestyle. Set a commitment of when you will dedicate prayer and fasting. This could look like fasting once a week for a few months or fasting frequently throughout the entire year. You could also consider dedicating a week every month for the year. Or you could set up a 21-day fast bi-monthly. Implement a fast that will challenge you. Be led by the Holy Spirit when setting a specific time frame. It's much easier to follow God's leading than to force yourself into a regimen that you're not prepared for.

Abstain from eating certain foods during these times, but don't focus so much on the foods. Fasting and prayer is about focusing on relationship with God; feeding your spirit and denying your flesh. Remember that fasting without a spiritual feast of God's Word is starvation. So, intentionally dedicate time with God in studying His Word. Since your spirit is being fed, this sacred time enhances your ability to recall certain stories and scriptures. Remind God of His word as you are in prayer. You'd be amazed by what you find. Take delight in prayer and fasting by making the most out of it. I promise you won't regret it.

Beloved, if you take anything from this message, know that it is your faith in God that gives you the power to do the impossible.

By faith, you believe that God exists and that He is a rewarder of those who diligently seek Him (Hebrews 11:6).

It is by faith that God gives you the power to obtain wealth (Deuteronomy 8:18).

It is by faith that you are able to move mountains (Matthew 17:20).

I...Am Chosen

It is by grace that you have been saved through faith, not of yourself (Ephesians 2:8).

We have multiple scriptures stating that your faith in God makes you powerful. Now, use the Word of God to see your God-given power manifest in your life.

I...Am Blessed
Defeating Demonic Interceptions

Deuteronomy 28:2 NKJV

"And all these blessings shall come upon you and overtake you, because you obey the voice of the LORD your God:"

As a child, I remember when my mom would play gospel music throughout our home. One of the songs she'd frequently play was "We're Blessed" by Fred Hammond. It's a nice upbeat song that'll remind you that you are truly blessed. You should check it out. Hearing that song again in my spirit inspired me to look up the scripture that it is derived from - Deuteronomy 28:2-8. It's the story written about Israel's journey from Egypt to their Promised Land – Cannon. God had a lot to give His people. Reading that scripture made me well convinced that God desires to bless His people.

For as long as I can remember, I've felt the oppression of limitations from time to time. One moment I'd feel powerful and relentless. The next moment, I'd feel weak, burdened, and bound. One moment I'd have blessings flow like a river of favor streaming in my life. Next thing I know, I'm back to the basics. Like a clogged artery, my creative flow would feel blocked from streaming. Recently, I've noticed this pattern in my life. So, I took a moment to pray about it with the expectation of God exposing the problem. He's told me that the limitation of my blessing-flow is called a Demonic Interception. You know how in a game of football when the quarterback player on offense intends to throw the ball to his teammate, but the player of defense catches the ball instead? That is called an interception. **A Demonic Interception is when God intends to bless you and you are expecting to receive the blessing, but an evil principality blocks you from receiving the blessing.** It is the moment when something completely unexpected counteracts your blessing from manifesting.

A prime example that I will never forget was when I was in 1st Grade. I attended a Private School - Anointed Word Academy. Let me be honest with you here, I wasn't the best student behavioral-wise. I always seemed to end up in trouble. I had such bad news behind my name that I remember telling one of the teachers my dream of her being my mom. I will never forget her response. She said, "Well, that was a nightmare!"

During the school year we had cheerleading tryouts. I was finally chosen to participate in the cheerleading team at school. Right when we were going to the chapel to receive our cheerleading uniforms, me and a few other girls were walking together. One of the girls who I really didn't get along with faked an injury and lied on me saying that I tripped her. One of the older grade students that were assisting us were actually in the front of the line leading us to the chapel. She turned around, scolded me, and then took me back to the classroom. She reported the incident to my teacher who then put me in timeout. It was during the time of my life when I tried to be obedient that no one believed me since they knew how much of a trouble I was. Just when I was getting ready to receive my blessing, a Demonic Interception - a lie by an "enemy" - caused me to miss out on my blessing.

Avoiding Demonic Interceptions

I have a book of stories that I can share with you where an unavoidable Demonic Interception had occurred in my life. After recognizing this pattern, I asked God for wisdom and precise discernment to help me avoid these problems before they occur. He began to reveal to me that Demonic Interceptions can be avoided several ways. Just to list a few:

1.   **Avoid telling people about the vision and ideas that God gives you** – This is highly necessary when you are working on the beginning stages of a project when it is unnecessary to tell others what you are producing. Like when a woman is in her first trimester of pregnancy, her belly doesn't show her pregnancy. It is not until her second trimester that her belly shows and she begins to talk about her pregnancy with others. This is the same scenario that occurs when God births a vision and idea within you. Develop the vision and idea undercover until God says it is time to reveal.

2.   **Always obtain good credibility and favor with man** – Authentically develop the Fruits of the Spirit – love, joy, peace, forbearance, kindness, goodness, faithfulness, gentleness, and self-control. No one can blame you for wrong-doing if you are known to be a humble servant.

3.   **Avoid drama and gossip** – You may encounter people who love to talk negatively about others. But be the light in the group that brings moral excellence amongst others.

4.   **Respond in Love** – People will always try to find a way to diminish your character. Recognize the spirit that is operating in evil and respond in love. I remind myself to do the loving thing that your flesh doesn't want to do. Treat your enemies with kindness and authority over any conflict.

Now, there are Demonic Interceptions that are unpreventable where life just throws an obstacle your way as you are on the path of doing great things. This is normal polarity that can be resolved through prayer, patience, and persistent faith in God. Truth is, you're going to be faced with challenges that tests your patience. You're going to hear negative comments from those who disagree with your work. You're going to face judgement from people who do not agree with your ideas. You're going to hit a bump in the road where an unfavorable circumstance disturbs you. We can make up excuses for the enemy saying, "maybe it wasn't meant to be" to avoid conflict. However, we must open our eyes to notice when the enemy is in the way of us receiving our breakthrough! I am sick and tired of feeling defeated by the enemy. It makes me want to push harder for breakthrough when I know that God has an open door for me. Don't you not only confess your blessing, but receive your blessing? I sure do! If God is telling you that you are blessed, you should be able to see the manifestation of your blessings.

Responding to Conflict

The lesson that I've learned throughout all of my unpreventable Demonic Interceptions is how you respond to the conflict. You may not be able to control unpreventable circumstances. However, you are able to control your response to them. You have to know when to fight your battles. Every time conflict interrupts your peace, you are faced with the decision to either retaliate or resolve the issue cordially before the conflict intercepts your blessing. If you're not careful to respond the correct way, you can end up forfeiting your blessing. It's easy to react in your flesh. But, pray and seek God on the matter. Decrease and allow God to increase. React maturely to the situation. Remind yourself that you are a representation of God. Know that you are not fighting your battles against flesh and blood but against the evil authorities and principalities in heavenly places (Ephesians 6:12).

Remind yourself that your identity is made new in Christ. Therefore, you are not subject to respond to conflict in a worldly manner.

Inheriting the Blessings of God through Your Mindset

Another lesson that I've learned when it comes to inheriting God's blessings is that as new creatures in Christ, we must change our mindset in order to manifest the blessings of God. It is through our mind that we must become new, for the scripture of Romans 12:2 states:

"Be not conformed to this world: but be ye transformed by the renewing of your mind, that ye may prove what is that good, and acceptable, and perfect, will of God."

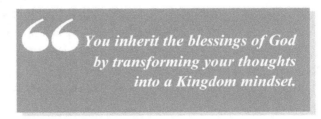

You inherit the blessings of God by transforming your thoughts into a Kingdom mindset.

It is through the transformation from thoughts of the defeat, thoughts of destruction, thoughts of poverty, thoughts of oppression, thoughts of limitation, to a mindset of the Kingdom of God that you are able to inherit the blessings of God. I've discovered that the more I dwell on my problems the more doubtful I become towards God's blessings. The more I listened to people who spoke pessimistically about situations the more I could never see myself as an overcomer. The more I pursued my own will the more I prevented myself from manifesting God's will. I'd gotten tired of being the lost cause who could never receive my blessings from God. I changed my mind by tuning into wisdom and concentrating on understanding. I stopped limiting myself to only hearing the Word of God, but also *doing* the Word of God. I began to look at scripture and speak scripture back to God.

I heard a Pastor preach on Matthew 17:20 where it states that we must have faith as small as a mustard seed in order to move mountains and nothing will be impossible. I took that message to heart at the perfect time where I was facing the seemingly impossible. I conjured up the confidence to continually trust in God no matter what conflict I was facing. Proverbs 18:21 states that there is death and life in the power of the tongue, and they that love it shall eat the fruit thereof. Well, I wanted good fruit to manifest in my life. So, I wrote down my mental mountains – debt, lack of finances, fear, and rejection to name a few – and I committed to speaking life over them every day and night. Little by little, I began to see the mountains move. My credit card was paid off. I received financial blessings. I became more and more fearless to pursue my purpose. I felt less rejected and more confident in life. I dedicated time to God at least an hour a day to spend time in His presence to hear from Him. I created declarations and affirmation which resulted in an improvement with my spiritual gifts. As a result, I recognized a shift in my thought process. Instead of hearing words that produced doubt, fear, and limitations, the Spirit of God was prophetically speaking through me on a continuous basis. I was truly experiencing the revelation of John 6:63 in my life where it is written,

"It is the spirit that quickeneth; the flesh profiteth nothing: the words that I speak unto you, they are spirit, and they are life."

Because I decided to change my mindset and allowed God to renew a major part of my heart, I inherited blessings. Over the course of seven months, God blessed me to join a Writer's Retreat where I have a long-term friendship with a wonderful group of girls who understand my uniquely designed lifestyle – a blessing that I've always desired. God has opened doors for me to sit in rooms with prominent people. Since I am continuously renewing my mind with the Word of God, I've been blessed to live in my own apartment after living in twelve different places over the past two years! God has been so faithful to fulfill His promises and blessings. I wouldn't have been able to inherit my blessings with my old doubtful mindset.

As you can see from my testimony, God's Word is true. When we commit to renewing our mindset with the revelation of His Word by faith, we get to experience a new and greater form of life for ourselves. It's not only the Demonic Interceptions that prevent our blessing-flow, but it is also our train of thought and the words that comes from the heart that has the ability to block blessings.

We have to do as Proverbs 4:23 states, "Keep your heart with all diligence, for out of it springs the issues of life." Let alone, Luke 6:45 states, "A good man out of the good treasure of his heart brings forth good; and an evil man out of the evil treasure of his heart brings forth evil. For out of the abundance of the heart his mouth speaks" (NKJV). What is in the treasure of your heart that is causing you to bring forth evil? Allow God to deal with you in the areas that are preventing you from receiving your blessings, my friend. He truly wants to bless you beyond your wildest dreams!

I...Am Made New

Dying to Your Former Self to Become the New You

Colossians 3:1-4 NLT

*Since you have been raised to new life with Christ, **set your sights on the realities of heaven**, where Christ sits in the place of honor at God's right hand. Think about the things of heaven, not the things of earth. For you died to this life, and your real life is hidden with Christ in God. And when Christ, who is your life, is revealed to the whole world, you will share in all his glory.*

There are moments where you can sense a shift occurring in your life. It may draw you into desiring to push everything and everyone away. However, there comes a time in metamorphosis where you must know how to morph into the new you with people around you. It's a part of what I call mastering the art of transformation. I'm not saying that it is okay to hold onto friendships that are causing you destruction in your faith in Christ. Anything that becomes a stumbling block to your faith will require you to let go. Handle the current season with maturity. Discern the level of isolation that you are within. Be mindful of any deception that the enemy tries to trap you in because isolation can sometimes lead to depression if not handled correctly. When God separates you from among others, He does this to consecrate you. It is a sign that He is performing an extremely new thing within you. He is refining you during your process. Notify an accountable friend to let them know that God is working on you and you need some time away to focus. If they don't understand or disagree with your decision, then they're not meant to participate in the cultivation that God is doing in your life at that moment.

Adjusting to your new image in Christ takes a mature step of faith even if it feels like you're stepping into faith alone. This is a move where you will need confidence in the Word of God. It will become your bread of life. It will become your stream of living waters. The new image that God is developing within you will require fasting and prayer, strength and dignity, wisdom and power, confidence and fearlessness. You must believe in yourself in this next level. Your mindset can't be set on yesterday's troubles, your energy cannot be given to everybody. Truth is, people will see your powerful development and will want all of it. But you must discern who they are and what their purpose is in your life.

Dying to your former self to become the new you can be taken a little harsh for some people. Not everyone thinks of death to self as a good thing. It takes a mature believer to understand the depth of dying to self. We are human beings with an utter compassion to pursue the desires of the flesh. We want to feel good, look good, and be good. We want what we want. We want our own way, period. If I can be honest, I have struggled to die to myself numerous times. There have been times when God would command me to wake up at 5 AM to get my day started with Him. Early mornings are not my best time of the day. I love to sleep in. Especially on cold winter mornings. I like to toss my covers over my head and soak in the doze of dawn. I oversleep so much that I have moments where I'd press snooze unconsciously recognizing that I've pressed snooze! Have you ever done that before? I have to set about five alarms on my phone; each one set thirty minutes apart to ensure that I WAKE UP. Death to self is a part of becoming the new you. Death can feel gruesome. But really, it's not as bad when you don't focus on the dying aspect. There is beauty that comes out of it all. Like when gold is tested by fire, it is refined into pure gold. Likewise, the death to yourself is tested in the furnace, forming your character into humility (1 Peter 1:7, emphasis added).

There are other ways that God will guide you into becoming the new you. You've already been renewed in Christ when you received salvation. However, that is not where the renewal of yourself stops. Receiving salvation is actually the beginning of the renewal of yourself. There are some Believers who haven't fully grasped the concept of Christianity after they've received Jesus as their Lord Savior and welcomed Him into their heart. Christianity is a faith walk where we cultivate a spiritual marriage with God. Just like any marriage in the natural, there is a growing process that comes within the relationship. A relationship requires unity - becoming one and growing together. You grow through trial and error, getting to know each other, spending quality time together, producing life together. The ultimate outcome of any relationship is learning to love in spite of one's flaws and imperfections and through any occurrence in life.

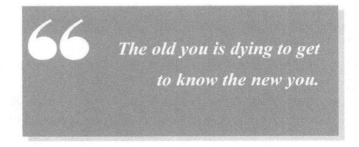

The old you is dying to get to know the new you.

Notice the Signs of Transformation

The signs that reveal God's call for transformation within your life is when:

- You sense a longing for change.
- You will develop a desire to feast on God's Word.
- You may end up changing jobs.
- New relationships form.
- New ideas develop.
- You feel the need to change your wardrobe.
- You begin to sense God tugging on you to go deeper within your prayer life.
- You begin to notice a part of your character needs more pruning to become more Christ-like.
- An unusual call to fasting and prayer, or frequent fasting and prayer.

There are various signs that signal your season of transition. As an entrepreneur, I'm currently witnesses transition on another level of my understanding. I want to encourage you if you are an entrepreneur. The life of an entrepreneur is a completely different world from the norm. The normal lifestyle that you are accustomed to dies at first hand. Hands down, you must transition out of your old way of thinking, doing, perceiving, speaking, acting, and living. When God calls you to pursue entrepreneurship, a new level of understanding is unlocked within you. Your life changes. You must surround yourself around people who are in alignment with the same calling. The way of life for an entrepreneur is not the same to someone who is not an entrepreneur. You have sleepless nights sometimes. You make investments in products and services that you usually wouldn't make. You find ways of making money out of anything and everything. You have days where you will second guess your calling to entrepreneurship. You'll talk to yourself more than you ever have before. You're challenged to overcome your weakness and your fears. You'll be tempted to focus on reality rather than the things above. You must reprogram your mindset from average to abundance. Most of all, you are ultimately pushed outside of your comfort zone to experience God on another level of understanding. All attributes of entrepreneurship require you to die to your flesh daily. Most of all, you literally have to die to your old self to become the new you.

The same death occurs when you are walking by faith in Christ. Since you are cultivating relationship with God, He will give you instructions that will require you to tell your flesh "no". One of the most common ways that we are challenged to say no to our flesh is during a time of fasting and prayer. Fasting is where you will get the most discipline in denying your flesh. You're reminded daily to say no to the Chick-fil-a fries to instead say yes to the salad. What makes it worse is that you get invited to all the events where people can freely eat as they please during your time of fasting. I remember a time where I was challenged to fast with no food, just liquids for 7 days. I just so happened to attend an event during this fast where they served vegan food. Mind you, I adore vegan food! Everything looked well made. The fumes from the food filled the entire room. They placed the meal directly in front my face, asking me if I wanted a plate...multiple times. They asked, "Are you sure? You can take a plate to go." I knew I would have devoured that food had I brought it home with me. I had to resist the temptation and die to my flesh the entire night. I literally had to dwell on heavenly things to ignore the temptation to devour the food and sweets that were gleaming in my face. Thank God I passed that test! Just to add a side note, after completing that 7-day fast, I was launched into another level within my business filled with new strategy, wisdom, insight, and ideas.

You see, there's something about dying to yourself that gives you a greater return spiritually. He calls you to not conform to the pattern of this world, but to be transformed by the renewing of your mind so that you will be able to test and approve His good, pleasing, and perfect will (Romans 12:2). God honors your obedience to follow His will. He sets you a part from others so that He can do greater works within you. As a chosen one, you will face challenges to come out from amongst others to walk in the image of Christ. He knows you are capable of carrying out His will because He created you and He believes in you more than you know.

I always recommend fasting and praying when you sense the tug to transition. Especially when you are seeking to become the new being that you've always wanted to become. During that particular transition, make it a habit to fast and pray for a lengthy period of time. Commit to a 21-day fast, 30-day fast, or 40-day fast. Statistics states that training your body, mind, and soul to develop new habits over longer period of days are proven to be successful. I've obtained great results of mental discipline from proactively meditating on the Word of God and applying healthier habits to my life during 21 days and 40 days of fasting. Is the process easy? Not at all, my friend. You must be determined to see change. You must put your faith in God and rely on His strength. It's like pushing yourself to exercise your body consistently to lose weight. The beginning of the process is challenging, the middle is rough, but the end result is worth every sweat, tear, and fight you've put into becoming the new you. I guarantee you that if you implement healthy habits – spiritually, mentally, and/or physically - on a consistent basis, you will receive the astonishing results you are looking for.

I...Am Healed
No Longer Wounded

Luke 6:45 NLT

A good person produces good things from the treasury of a good heart, and an evil person produces evil things from the treasury of an evil heart. What you say flows from what is in your heart.

Declare this aloud with me: I Am Healed!
Shout it again: I Am Healed!
One more time. This time shout it from the depth of your soul: I Am Healed! Receive it. Feel it. Embrace it.

We may not share the same exact story. However, I believe that somewhere in your heart you needed to declare this statement today. Healing is a journey that not many people can fathom. It is a common need, yet subtle accomplishment for some of us who have dealt with lifelong wounds. If I can be transparent with you, my friend, I am struggling to write this message. This subject on healing is one of the very last messages that I'm writing. It's been placed in a category of questions that I've asked God to help me overcome countless times. What's crazy is that He's told me that healing is my portion. Hence, I must receive it. I must submit to it. I must embrace it. I must claim it as mine.

Healing is a valuable part of your identity. Healing is necessary for your health and your growth. If you're still wounded, you can end up in a cycle of broken relationships with broken people more times than desired. You may wonder why you are attracting the things and the people that you are trying to break free from. Well first off, scripture states that a good person produces good things from the treasury of a good heart, and an evil person produces evil things from the treasury of an evil heart. What you say flows from what is in your heart. (Luke 6:45 NLT). So, if your heart is filled with brokenness and negative thinking and you are constantly speaking negatively over your life, then you will cause yourself to bring forth negative things. You are attracting the things that you don't desire because somewhere in your heart, you are festering a treasure of brokenness. And you need God to heal you from this heavy spirit so that you can produce life-giving things.

Let That Junk Go!

One of the most effective mechanisms to healing is forgiving others who you feel have wronged you. Forgive yourself for allowing it to get the best of you. And receive your forgiveness from God. Forgiveness is the key that unlocks the doors of healing. You can never heal if you're still festering the thought of how your step-mom used to abuse you growing up as a child. Do you know that holding on to family-dysfunction distorts the expectation you may have amongst the people you will meet in your future? Statistics state that children who grow up without a father can experience emotional dysfunctions that can cause one or more of these effects in their life: aggression, silent anger, depression, low self-esteem, do poorly in schools, use drugs, or be incarcerated. I've noticed a few of these emotional dysfunctions within one of my close family members. I see the life that he's living and it breaks my heart to notice this unhealthy cycle within my bloodline.

These dysfunctional wounds that we carry. They tear our lives a part. As if we've been tarrying in the marriage to our parents' broken hearts. They've been unaware of its existence. We've developed these wounds from the way our peers used and abused us. We've sought to dissipate these wounds with false love, artificial drugs, and hugs from the arms of strangers. We've searched scriptures and looked to God to find the answers. Not knowing that Jesus is the healing, our ultimate answer...We've been overthinking.

Witnessing the effects of fatherlessness or any form of family dysfunction gives me a longing to help people cultivate a healthy relationship with Abba, our Heavenly Father. It's difficult to carry the weight that comes with unforgiveness, shame, anger, bitterness, depression, and such unhealthy emotions. Mental dysfunction is one of the many unhealthy emotions that prevents healing from taking place. There are many people who've carried unhealthy emotional weights within their spirit, not knowing the freedom and life that comes with having a relationship with God through Christ Jesus. It's not until the dysfunctional spirit is confronted where deliverance can occur. One must be willing to receive deliverance from the dysfunctional spirit in order to be healed. If they don't want deliverance, then the dysfunctional spirit will linger until they're ready to be healed.

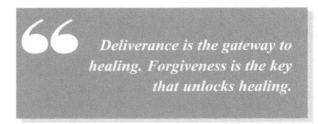

> *Deliverance is the gateway to healing. Forgiveness is the key that unlocks healing.*

Deliverance

I have this habit of sensing a need for deliverance within myself. Let's get RAW and REAL. I'm not gonna to act like I don't have issues that only God can deliver me from. I'm walking faith to faith, glory to glory. So, all judgement I cast aside. What I love about deliverance is that in the very moment, I sense God's deep desire to make me whole. Every time I experience deliverance, I feel like weights have been lifted from my shoulders. I feel like I've been healed. I'm more joyful than I was before. I gain a lot of energy to complete assignments. The very things that I needed God to deliver me from were renounced.

What makes deliverance effective is when you willingly receive deliverance. You may be suffering from depression, fear, oppression, lust, anger, offense, etc., yet you want to be free. The question that I have for you is this: *Are you truly ready to receive deliverance?* There is a process to deliverance. You have to be willing to fight past the comfort zone of your flesh even when you don't feel like submitting to the deliverance process. Many people often receive the laying on of hands and are set free in their spirit. Unlike most physical deliverance where one is set free from a physical infirmity such as tumors, paralysis, or physical pain, spiritual deliverance requires ones to be ministered to before and after their deliverance encounter. A minister can lay hands on you and cast demons out. However, if you are not properly filled afterwards, you can fall back into the same old habits.

I encourage you to allow God to examine your heart as He molds and shapes you into His image. Allow Him to renew your entire life. The process to healing can get pretty ugly. However, it is necessary as you walk within this faith walk. I'll let you know up front what to expect. The enemy is going to doubt you. He's going to turn people against you. You're going to feel uncomfortable as the spirits within you are confronted. All of this is a part of the deliverance process. Throughout your process, spend time cultivating your relationship with the Lord. Deliverance is a vulnerable and sacred place. The beauty of deliverance is that you have broken through obstacles that were seemingly impossible to break.

I want you to imagine what your future will hold when you are renewed within your mind. You'll embrace freedom in levels you've never experienced before. You'll find yourself greeting strangers even though you weren't greeting-friendly before. You'll cultivate long-term healthy relationships. You'll find new ways to discipline yourself. You'll experience breakthrough in various areas of your life – financially, spiritually, mentally, physically. As you already know, the enemy doesn't want you to experience this new lifestyle of freedom. Don't be your own worst enemy. Seek God for healing. Don't be afraid to get therapy or counseling if you feel you need it. Therapy and counseling is a deeper form of healing from traumatic circumstances from your past. It is God's desire for you to make a final decision to let that junk go!

I...Am Forgiven

Letting Go of the Weight of Condemnation

Romans 8:1 NKJV

There is therefore now no condemnation to those who are in Christ Jesus, who do not walk according to the flesh, but according to the Spirit.

Quite often, we find scripture based on forgiveness where God teaches us to forgive one another. Well, what about when God forgives us? How do we know we are forgiven? I've questioned God countless times about how to write this chapter of the book because I already understand the lesson in forgiving others, and I understood that God has already forgiven me of my sins. But I've struggled to fully grasp the concept of how to teach it to you effectively without rambling on in sentences. So, here I am. God has given me wisdom to share with you on the topic of forgiveness in the area of condemnation.

When I think of forgiveness, I think about many people in the body of Christ who've lived years with the spirit of condemnation. It makes me wonder, if Christians are dealing with the spirit of condemnation, then how many nonbelievers are avoiding Christianity because of it? I've done street evangelism, even talked with a few of my family members about their views towards Christianity. Do you want to know the most common answer I hear? They say, "I don't want anything to do with Christianity. All Christians do is judge me." I also hear, "Christians are hypocrites. They can't help me with my problems if they're doing wrong too." My cousin recently told me, "I'm not ready to give my life to God. I can't come to Him the way that I am." You know what I sense out of all of these responses? I sense a spirit of condemnation.

There are people suffering in sin, afraid to come to Jesus because they are weighed down by condemnation. I listen to their stories of how they used to attend church. They say they couldn't find the help they needed from the church. Or they say the people in the church weren't living the right examples. I'm not saying that this is okay. Maybe they've had horrible experiences. But the way the church appears should not affect one's relationship with God. Although it is necessary for new believers in Christ to have healthy examples of salvation, still, no one should lose their relationship with God based on what they see in church.

Condemnation appears in various forms. It paralyzes one's faith, influencing the lie of unforgiveness or even rejection. It can also cause unworthiness of receiving Jesus as Lord and Savior. Condemnation ultimately prevents believers and nonbelievers from living in the spirit of our Lord Jesus Christ.

Receiving God's forgiveness liberates you from the grave of oppression that your soul has been buried in. Like carrying pounds of rotten produce, God's people have purchased lies from rejection's deceptions. We must get to the bottom of condemnation so that we can receive God's unconditional love through forgiveness.

Stand Up, Pick Up Your Mat, and Go Home

The biblical message about Jesus healing the paralytic who was brought through the roof of His home is an astounding example of how we are to receive forgiveness and never let condemnation deter us. Let's read the scripture:

Luke 5:17-26 NLT

17 One day while Jesus was teaching, some Pharisees and teachers of religious law were sitting nearby. (It seemed that these men showed up from every village in all Galilee and Judea, as well as from Jerusalem.) And the Lord's healing power was strongly with Jesus. 18 Some men came carrying a paralyzed man on a sleeping mat. They tried to take him inside to Jesus, 19 but they couldn't reach him because of the crowd. So they went up to the roof and took off some tiles. Then they lowered the sick man on his mat down into the crowd, right in front of Jesus. 20 Seeing their faith, Jesus said to the man, "Young man, **your sins are forgiven**." 21 But the Pharisees and teachers of religious law said to themselves, "Who does he think he is? That's blasphemy! Only God can forgive sins!" 22 Jesus knew what they were thinking, so he asked them, "Why do you question this in your hearts? 23 Is it easier to say 'Your sins are forgiven,' or 'Stand up and walk'? 24 **So I will prove to you** that the Son of Man has the authority on earth to forgive sins." Then Jesus turned to the paralyzed man and said, "**Stand up, pick up your mat, and go home**!" 25 And immediately, as everyone watched, the man jumped up, picked up his mat, and went home praising God. 26 Everyone was gripped with great wonder and awe, and they praised God, exclaiming, "We have seen amazing things today!"

Jesus initially performed an invisible miracle forgiving the man's sins. But to prove that He had authority on earth to forgive sins, He provided a visible miracle of healing the man's body. Jesus provided visible proof that the man was forgiven because the Pharisees were doubting this man's deliverance. The man was living proof that Jesus has the authority to heal and forgive. This entire story was provided for us so that we may receive the healing and forgiveness that Jesus has already given us. It is up to us to receive it. Once we receive healing and forgiveness, Jesus tells us to do 3 things: 1) Stand Up 2) Pick Up Your Mat 3) Go Home.

1. Stand Up: Verse 25, "And immediately, as everyone watched, the man jumped up,"

Arise! Wake up to the liberty that is in Christ Jesus. Whom the Son sets free is free indeed (John 8:36). The brokenness that you've battled with can no longer weigh you down. Arise! For you were not created to remain bound to limitations. Arise to the authority that is instilled within your God-identity. Awaken to the bountiful land of wisdom, power, and fertility that God desires to restore within you. When you stand up, don't lie back down on the very thing(s) you've been paralyzed to. Pick up what kept you bound and walk.

2. Pick Up Your Mat: Verse 25, "picked up his mat,"

God says to pick up condemnation, bitterness, lustful desires, gluttony, shame, unforgiveness, jealousy, fear, doubt, poverty, insecurity, depression, etc. Pick up what has overtaken you. Pick up what you've been settling for. You've been convinced by lies that you would forever be bound to your mat. You thought you would never give your heart to the Lord. You look around every day to see poverty written all over your life. You lied with fear that has held you hostage, literally sucking the life out of your faith. But God says, "Pick it up!" Your "mat" doesn't have authority over you, beloved. You have authority over it. You were meant to stand on your mat. Your mat is the testimony you carry as evidence that God is your Deliverer. You have a testimony to share about how God healed you and forgave you of your sins. So, rejoice in your freedom!

3. Go Home: Verse 25, "and [he] went home praising God."

This man rejoiced in his liberty. You can do the same. Rejoice! Praise God! Like inhaling the fresh aroma of lavender's essence, intake God's freedom into the depth of your soul. Now that you know what God has done for you, go and tell others. Go to your church home. Get plugged in. When you've been delivered from anything, it is vital that you fill up with the word, wisdom, and knowledge of God. Like the Pharisees that condemned Jesus, the enemy is going to send ways to condemn you again. He's always seeking whom he can devour to drag them back into their sin.

Surround yourself around faithful believers who will hold you accountable. If you do not have a church home, I encourage you to ask God to lead you to a trustworthy house of God that is fitting for you. A church that is Christ-centered. A pastor that preaches sound doctrine. A church where you belong. A church where you can call home. Trust me, I understand the difficulty of finding a well-committed, trustworthy church home.

If you're having a hard time finding one, cultivate your relationship with Jesus in your own home. Of course, God knows you'd like community and fellowship. There are numerous churches you can find online as well. Get plugged in and always test the spirit of what you hear and see. God will always give you discernment on where to call home.

If you are new to the body of Christ, I highly recommend finding a church home. To be fresh out of the world without any brothers or sisters of the faith to hold you accountable can be tough. A lot of backlash and temptation occurs during transition. Hence, surround yourself with people in a church home. It's always the safest place to be.

Release the Weight, Receive Forgiveness

One of the greatest things I love about God's forgiveness is that He doesn't hold our sins against us. This is a concept that we must understand in order to walk in complete freedom. I've committed countless sins, and for the longest, I held onto the thought that I was still bound to unforgiveness. Even though I knew God had forgiven me, I longed for confirmation of His forgiveness.

I'll share a secret with you that I'm not at all proud of. It still touches me when I think about it. But it's okay. The outcome of the situation reminds me to never fall back into the temptation again. I feel as though what I'm about to share with you is necessary to share because you may be one of the many women who've had the same encounter, but you're still grieving condemnation every time you think of it. For the man reading this book, you're permitted to peruse this portion if you'd like. You may find this story relatable. Be led by the Lord. Just know that I've come to help set you free, my friend.

*Takes a deep breath. There was a time in my life where I had broken my celibacy vow with God. I mean, intentionally broke it with no care of love in my heart about keeping my body for God anymore. I was at a point in my relationship with God, where I felt as if He was far away. I was growing weary and weak, desiring God to fulfill my heart's desires. I couldn't hear God clearly for direction. You know those moments when you're entertaining someone even though God told you he/she was a distraction? Well, I was talking to a guy that God commanded me to let go of. I'll call him Kevin for confidentiality. I claimed myself "ministering" to Kevin, helping him to receive salvation. I knew he was attracted to me. I also knew he wanted one thing. I ignored the thought of us even getting that far in our "situationship". God told me to stop responding to his text messages. I, of course, didn't want to be rude and cut him off. I was too friendly.

Pulling away from Kevin grew harder for me, the more I indulged in conversation. He'd buy me dinner, we'd play pool, he had a fancy luxurious car. He was entertaining my sweet spot. Next thing you know, he kissed me. I knew right there I was in BIG trouble. Kevin was buying me things and invited me over to his crib. He even asked me to cook for him. All along, I sensed my connection with God started fading. It was difficult for me to receive a response from God for my life with guilt in my heart.

On one particular Sunday morning, Lord knew what that day would hold. I went to church, hoping for God to quench the thirst in my spirit. But after service, I felt emotionally wiped out. As if a leaching spirit sucked the blood of Jesus out of my life, I was empty, unfulfilled, and lowly in spirit. Now when I think of it, what if God was waiting for me to repent – to turn to Him to receive the breakthrough that I was seeking? I was expecting *God* to move for me, even though I hadn't obediently moved first. It's not like I didn't know that I was walking in disobedience by talking to the guy that God told me to let go of.

That same exact Sunday after service, I remember clear as day, I was selfishly plotting to rebel because God wasn't moving for *me*. God wasn't removing my battle with the sexual urges and hormones as I wanted Him to. He had already given me a way out. God gave me signs revealing that Kevin was not good for me. He told me to stop all forms of communication. God didn't end the communication because He had given me a **choice**, and He believed that I was capable of saying no to sin.

On the way home from Sunday's service, I texted Kevin to see if he was available. I told him I'd cook for him. I made my specialty oven-baked succulent salmon and mixed peppers with a side of steamed broccoli and rice. I drove to Kevin's apartment with all intentions to give him what he wanted. I slightly anticipated what I was getting myself into. But I brushed off all hesitation before walking to his door. I walked into his home with thoughts lingering in the back of my mind, "Should I just go home? What am I doing?" On the other hand, I was hearing, "Just stay. You're here anyway. Get it over with." I proceeded to engage in conversation with Kevin, signaling where to take things from there. I saw red flags and signals all around his bedroom, letting me know the kind of guy he is. The most significant sign that stood out to me was the condom wrappers on his closet floor. When I asked him about it he told me some story. I asked him when was the last time he had sex. He said, "About three months ago. Why?"…*blank face* LIES from the pit of hell! Who has condom wrappers on their bedroom floor for three months? Major bad sign! But I was too stubborn to walk out. I knew that that day would be the only day I'd give up. I felt that I needed to get that urge out of me. I didn't want to go to God to ask Him to take the urge away and feel unfulfilled again. My flesh was too weak at that point. My entire soul – my mind, my will, and my emotions – was in a gridlock of confusion and loneliness. I should have let Kevin go in the beginning when God told me that the spirit he carried was seeking to corrupt my purity.

I broke my covenant with God that day. I decided that I was absolutely not proud of. Moments after Kevin and I's encounter, I felt the worse pain in my spirit. As if someone reached into the depth of my stomach to set my intestines on fire, I felt the grieving of the Holy Spirit take over me. I ran to the bathroom sobbing and screaming into a towel uncontrollably on the floor. I repeatedly screamed, "What have I done?!" I heard Kevin knocking on the door to ask if I was okay. I just needed a moment alone to process everything. I gathered myself together, and before I could leave, I noticed Kevin's concern. He didn't understand what just happened and I felt too ashamed to tell him. He walked me out of the door. I went home. I spent the remainder of that evening lying in bed, wrestling to go to sleep with tears in my eyes. I felt that God was disappointed with me even after I had repented. I couldn't forgive myself for allowing myself to go that far with rebellion.

Days after my encounter with Kevin, fear invaded my spirit. I was convinced that I might have had HIV. I experienced night sweats frequently. I had menstrual cramps with no menstrual cycle. I also experienced irregular hormones which caused me to think I might have been pregnant. I was thinking, "What if people find out that I have HIV? What would people think of me if I were pregnant? I can't have this guy's kids! He's not even my husband!" Isn't it crazy how fear torments you from one single sign that reveals something is off? Fear had its way in my mind! Of course, searching for HIV symptoms and pregnancy signs online made the anxiety worse. All that I was experiencing had driven me to pray fervently against the assumption that I might have had HIV or could have possibly been pregnant. After a while, my body felt normal again. But what hadn't changed was my mind.

I remember feeling depressed for a while. I battled with condemnation, badly. I thought God was disappointed with me. I felt as if receiving my purposed husband was canceled due to my disobedience. How could I get back on one accord with God again? I knew that I needed a change. But how could I change? The change that I needed was not only to receive forgiveness from God but also to forgive myself. I had already acknowledged my sin and repented for it. I just needed to learn how to forgive myself. Reading the Bible was my only hope to turn to for help. I was way too ashamed to talk to my friends and family. The Lord was my only Teacher, Healer, and Deliverer during the time. Even in me seeking for forgiveness through Christ alone, He saw fit to send people to talk with me about my struggle. You see, holding this guilt and shame within me was unhealthy for my spirit. So, God used the people around me who understood my mistake. I was able to vent privately with my coworkers in the middle of our girl's night out. Thankfully, they didn't judge me. They were surprised that I'd do such a thing, but one of the girls completely understood and gave me biblical wisdom and encouragement. They both helped me laugh it all off. I was also open to vent to my photographer. He encouraged me to receive that God isn't mad at me and that I needed to forgive myself. Out of the many kind words he expressed, he told me not to allow condemnation to get the best of me because God has ultimately given me freedom through Christ.

As you can see, God didn't let me suffer in my thoughts alone. There was something about venting that gave me a peace of mind. Perhaps talking about my problem opened up the opportunity for me to receive self-forgiveness. Let alone, scripture such as Isaiah 41:13 confirmed His presence:

"For I hold you by your right hand—I, the Lord your God. And I say to you, 'Don't be afraid. I am here to help you."

Scripture such as Isaiah 40:31 confirmed His strength:

"But they that wait upon the Lord shall renew their strength; they shall mount up with wings as eagles; they shall run, and not be weary; and they shall walk, and not faint."

Do you see how our gracious Heavenly Father has a special way of revealing His unconditional love and forgiveness to His children? He knows your struggles. He knows when you're going to make a mistake. Like me, you may have been convinced in various ways to believe the lie that God holds your sins against you. Scriptures states in Isaiah 43:25 that God blots out your transgressions for His own sake and remembers your sins no more (emphasis added). This lets you know that God has already forgiven you even though you may not have made the necessary sacrifices to honor Him. Though there are repercussions that comes with disobedience, God is gracious enough restore.

Repentance

If you haven't done this already, I encourage you to practice repentance. Repentance is not a bad thing; it's a spiritual cleansing technique. You may be wondering, "Well if I'm already forgiven, why should I repent?" Repentance is an act of humility. It is acknowledging that you have done something unrighteous. It is an open confession to God that you do not intend to turn back to sin.

For instance, I've been told that I can come off blunt in conversations. I may say something that offends my brother or sister in Christ. Though something may be true about the person, my delivery can cause offense to grow in one's heart. When God reveals this problem to me, I acknowledge my wrong-doing. I repent, and I turn away.

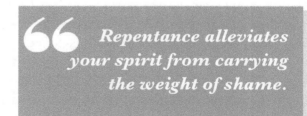

Repentance alleviates your spirit from carrying the weight of shame.

If we confess our sins, he is faithful and just and will forgive us our sins and purify us from all unrighteousness.
1 John 1:9 NIV

My friend, I want you to know that you are God's child. Daddy will never turn away from you in your wrong-doing. If anything, He desires you to run towards Him for shelter. If you get anything out of this message, I hope that it has given insight and understanding regarding God's forgiveness for you. You should never have to live with condemnation's scars. If you're battling with forgiveness, I want you to do yourself a favor, receive God's mercy and forgive yourself. Encourage yourself. Tell yourself I love you every day. Repent and never turn back. Do what you can to remove everything that would trigger the influence of sin you've dealt with. Fill your spirit with God's Word based on His love for you and your identity. Fast and pray. Find an accountability partner to help keep you encouraged. Move forward and don't look back. Most of all, I pray that you receive God's love, healing, forgiveness, and freedom over your life, beloved.

Before ending this chapter, I want to share with you a few scriptures that'll help you to not only receive God's forgiveness, but to also unravel the understanding of your God-identity.

If you're seeking satisfaction, healing, and forgiveness, meditate on Psalm 103:1-5 TPT.
With my whole heart, with my whole life,
and with my innermost being,
I bow in wonder and love before you, the holy God!
2 Yahweh, you are my soul's celebration.
How could I ever forget the miracles of kindness
you've done for me?
3 You kissed my heart with forgiveness, in spite of all I've done.
You've healed me inside and out from every disease.
4 You've rescued me from hell and saved my life.
You've crowned me with love and mercy.
5 You satisfy my every desire with good things.
You've supercharged my life so that I soar again
like a flying eagle in the sky!

If you're seeking to receive God's kindness, meditate on Psalm 103:8 TPT:

Lord, you're so kind and tenderhearted to those who don't deserve it and so patient with people who fail you! Your love is like a flooding river overflowing its banks with kindness.

If you're practicing discipline, meditate on Hebrews 12:11 NIV:

No discipline seems pleasant at the time, but painful.

Later on, however, it produces a harvest of righteousness and peace for those who have been trained by it.

If you are seeking gratitude and strength, meditate on Psalm 28:6-7 NLT:

Praise the Lord! For he has heard my cry for mercy.

7 The Lord is my strength and shield.

    I trust him with all my heart.

He helps me, and my heart is filled with joy.

    I burst out in songs of thanksgiving.

If you are seeking peace, meditate on Isaiah 26:3 NLT:

You will keep in perfect peace all who trust in you, all whose thoughts are fixed on you!

If you are seeking to affirm your victory, meditate on 1 John 4:4 and 1 John 5:4 AMP:

1 John 4:4 NKJV

You are of God, little children, and have overcome them, because He who is in you is greater than he who is in the world.

1 John 5:4 AMP

For everyone born of God is victorious and overcomes the world; and this is the victory that has conquered and overcome the world—our [continuing, persistent] faith [in Jesus the Son of God].

If you are seeking to maintain your authority over sin, meditate on Psalm 119:113 NKJV:
Direct my steps by Your word,
And let no iniquity have dominion over me.

If you are seeking to maintain purity, meditate on Psalm 51:10 NLJV:
Create in me a clean heart, O God,
And renew a steadfast spirit within me.

I…Am NOT Rejected

Deliverance from Broken Friendship Cycles

Romans 8:10 TPT

Now Christ lives his life in you! And even though your body may be dead because of the effects of sin, his life-giving Spirit imparts life to you because ***you are fully accepted by God***.

Rejection is topic that I can very much relate to. I've come to realize that rejection stems from abandoned relationships. Rejection can be derived from the effects of how someone made you feel. And it can become easy to feel abandoned, angry, disappointed, and hurt by people. If rejection is left unresolved, it can turn into a lingering effect of false assumptions upon others who aren't intending to reject you. The emotional effect of rejection is a sign that healing is needed.

> "
> *You should never make others feel the same pain that you feel towards them, because they will only remember the fact that you made them feel painful."*

Like most of us in the girl world, we've experienced a heart-breaking "break-up" whether with our ex-boyfriend, ex-fiancé, ex-husband, or ex-friend. We know what it's like to experience the pain of a what felt like a disconnect from an unbiblical chord. Depending on the reason behind the break up, your emotions can run into a whirlwind of emotions that are connected with the spirit of rejection. You conjure up thoughts that make you want to retaliate against them. You may even go as far as blocking the ex-friend off of your social media page. You might gossip with your other friends about them. But did you ever realize that gossip can plant bad seeds into someone else's heart about the person you're in disagreement with? At the end of the whole shebang, you never talked to your ex-friend about the problem you've had with her. You never hit her up to see what's going on in her world - how she's emotionally feeling, if she needed prayer, or why she's isolating herself. You made the whole situation all about you - how you've felt and how you believe you're being rejected. You've created false assumptions within your mind, believing in the whispers of the enemy that she's rejected you and wants nothing to do with you. This type of thinking is harmful and can cause destruction in your relationships.

As a kid growing up, I began this indifferent cycle of friendships where I'd have break-ups with friends. I constantly felt like an eight-ball on a pool table – I felt as though I was the odd ball that stood out from everyone in my classes. Though I wanted to be popular, I was desperate to be loved. I desired to be cool. I thought dressing up and looking cute would give me the attention that I wanted. But I struggled to keep healthy friendships. There was always something about me and other females that didn't connect during my Elementary to High School years. I remember making childish decisions that led to arguments. When a friend made me mad, I'd think of ways to make them feel the pain I was feeling. I had an episode where my "friends" wanted to fight me because I vented to another girl (whom I thought would keep things confidential) about how hurt I was by another friend. Due to my experiences with females, I questioned if I were meant to have female friends. Why couldn't me and the cool girls get along? Why were my friendships ending almost every school year? I wondered who could I truly trust? I hated my identity as the "different" girl. I didn't understand my purpose in life. It seemed like no matter what, I was going to end up with broken friendships.

Even up to my adulthood, I've experienced this same cycle. I've asked God:
Why can't I keep friendships?
Why do I feel rejected?
Why do people hold me accountable to reach out to them instead of having mutual contact?
How come my friends and family members won't call me?
Why can't I gain a higher following on social media?
When am I ever going to grow from the bottom to soar at the top?
This is the emotional effect that rejection can leave you with. It causes you to question yourself, as well as the people in your life. You hear more of rejection's assumptions rather than God's truth concerning your life. All of these questions and assumptions can hinder our confidence, and God wants to root them out.

When the spirit of rejection is left untreated in your soul for so long, you can go through phases of *expected temporary relationships* – expecting the friendship to be temporary from the start. Living with short-term friendships for so long can build walls of isolation, preventing new friends from getting to know you because you're already *expecting* them to break you a part. The break-up cycle can cause guilt and shame to arise if you linger in the assumption that you were the cause of your last break-up. So then guilt and shame creates distance because you fear that you will hurt the new friends in your life.

If you're reading this and you know you can relate, I encourage you to know that this cycle of broken relationships and the spirit of rejection has no authority over your life! One thing I've discovered to be true is that wherever opposition has fought you the most, it is the very area where you will make a huge impact in life. It scares you to know that the area of your life where you've felt incapable, disqualified, unaccomplished, let down, belittled, and rejected is the biggest blessing within your purpose. The enemy tried to take you out with all of the chaos between you and the people in your life. But did you know that you've survived every victimized situation because you were made to be a victor over relationships? Yes, indeed you are!

There's a victor in your soul that takes relationships seriously. You're the woman who sees the heart of man and does what she can to serve people with love. You're the man who is okay with working behind the scenes because you're not hungry for the spotlight. You have a tender heart to passionately care for others. You delight in giving back to others because you know what it's like to have the *least* of the last.

The adversary is going to always try to tear apart your relationships. How you handle the battle is relevant to your maturity in being responsible for the other relationships that God places in your life. Every leader has to deal with broken relationships. There is a leader of some sort within you, chosen one. God knows how much you can handle. He knows who to place in your life. He knows how may relationships you can handle in a season. He ultimately knows your purpose. So, Lord knows that you were built to make a positive impact on people's lives. The enemy wants you to get angry, frustrated, and rejected by the people in your life. But I come to tell you that you do not have to fester with the frustrations of bitterness. You were created to love your neighbor as yourself. You were created to love the Lord your God with all of your heart, mind, and soul. And you cannot love with the best of your ability if you have a spiritual community of rejection controlling your emotions within your relationships. Let me break this down for you.

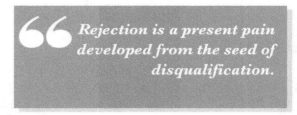

Rejection is a present pain developed from the seed of disqualification.

Somewhere along the line of your past, you've strongly felt the following emotions due to a broken relationship:

- Unworthiness
- Unacceptance
- Isolation
- Abandonment
- Denial
- Pronounced Unqualified
- Inferiority
- Disapproval
- Loneliness
- Ignored
- Neglect
- Forgotten
- Forsaken

If somewhere along the line of your past you've felt any of the adjectives listed above, and you still feel this way at times, this reveals that you haven't been emotionally healed in the area of rejection. You have this hidden pain within your heart that has become numb over the years. You're wondering why you have cycles of broken relationships. Evermore, now that you've grown your relationship with God, your perspective has broadened to discover that you have this undesired pain towards an ex-friend whom you never settled a disagreement with. So, what are you going to do? Suppress the feeling of rejection and continue to live with the assumption that your ex-friend is the cause of your pain? Or are you going to go before the throne of God and allow Him to give you wisdom on how to settle the problem?

The Silent Escape

Can I be transparent with you? I can confess that I've been used to silently escaping friendships. A silent escape is just as similar to the silent treatment. Unlike the silent treatment where you'd temporarily distance yourself from someone, a silent escape is when you'd permanently remove yourself from someone's life. This sounds really bad, but I'd silently escape friendships. I just had the expectation that some mistake I made would end the friendship. So, to avoid heartbreak and the girl drama, I'd end the friendship in my heart before they could even approach me. Growing up in high school, I'd give friends the silent treatment because I'd assume that we've both moved on. Anyone who has dealt with broken friendships knows all about the silent treatment and can testify that they've done it before. Am I proud of it? Absolutely not. Silent escapes do not always do justice. Like leaving an open wound without coverage, it often times causes unresolved issues in one's heart. There are some friendships that God has destined you to keep, but your silent escapes can speak a louder volume of contradiction that could be avoided if you'd handle the situation properly.

Through my healing process, God reminded me of a close friend that I went to high school with. We stayed connected ever since. Never went too long without speaking to each other. During my transition to Georgia in 2019, it seemed as if our friendship was completely splitting a part. I was well convinced that he thought I was no longer relevant in his life. Being my overanalytical self, I noticed that he unfollowed me on Facebook but still kept me as a friend. He unfollowed me on Instagram, he even unfriended me on the Bible App. I didn't receive a phone call or conversational text message to discuss what the issue was. I was convinced that he didn't want anything to do with me. So, within my heart, I blocked him and intentionally made up in my mind that he deserved the silent escape, FOREVER.

There goes rejection again, messing around with my heart. I was already losing people that I considered close to me. Hence, realizing that the guy that hung around in my life longer than any other guy had hurt me the most by seemingly escaping my life. I wanted not only my friend to feel my pain, but I wanted everyone who were escaping my life to feel my pain. Within this matter, God corrected my heart towards my loss of friends. God told me these very words, *"You should never make others feel the same pain that you feel towards them, because they will only remember the fact that you made them feel painful."* Though I had made up in my mind that I was going to give my guy friend the silent escape, God continued to place him on my mind. As if God was questioning if I truly wanted to let him go. I had to humble myself to realize that this particular friend is someone that could potentially be a lifelong friend. This was the guy that I helped reconcile his relationship with Christ. This was the guy that kicked it with me at the beach. The guy that I'd always hang with when I visited home in Florida. This was the guy that I could laugh hysterically with. This was a friendship where we knew each other enough to be completely transparent with each other and forgive one another. This was the only friendship where we've never argued. God reminded me to harden not my heart, but to instead, love in spite of...

Expired Friendships

Now, there are times where friendships have expiration dates. It's just that seasons have changed. There could be various reasons as to why the friendship has ended. God could be shifting your environment. Or perhaps you're going through spiritual transformation. You come to a point where the person or persons you've been hanging tightly with are no longer meant to be a part of your inner circle. It is necessary to let them know that you have to move forward to grow mentally and spiritually. Now, a good friend would understand this and she wouldn't prohibit your growth. If your friends are trying to keep you conformed to the old you, let them go. God created you so that you may conform into the likeness of Jesus Christ. This means you were created to grow, to become the best version of yourself through your purpose in life. Anyone who stunts your growth is controlled by a spirit of manipulation. Pray for their deliverance and follow God's will for your life.

How to Heal from the Cycle of Broken Relationships and Rejection?

When you don't deal with the seed of rejection, you begin to assume that the people in your life have the potential of disqualifying you. These assumptions occur based off of the emotional impact that you were left with from one of your former friendships. Rejection recognizes itself and starts to build a community of disqualification within your soul. It sees Sister Abandonment and rides along with her. Then they start gossiping about Unworthiness. They feed Inferiority in the back seat of your mind. Makes a U-turn to your past to pick up Neglect. Forsakes the emotion that's been lingering in labor, giving birth to Isolation. Due to the trauma of Intimidation, you feel Loneliness shadowing you. So, here you are with this jungle of rejection collaborating within your soul that is causing you problems with your past, current, and future relationships. You're wondering, how in God's name do you heal from this cycle of broken relationships and rejection?

As we know, ***rejection is a present pain that has been developed from the seed of disqualification.*** This is caused by the likelihood of the repetitious pessimism that you or someone have spoken over your life. Pessimism may sound like,

"You'll never be enough",

"Nobody likes you",

"Marriage never worked out in our family. So, you'll never get married."

For the woman reading this, perhaps a pessimistic mindset could have been developed through the repetitious cycle of being kicked out of a circle of friends. Or constant rejection from men. It could stem from constant failure or heavy criticism from leadership. For the man reading this, a pessimistic mindset could have been developed from the constant pressure of being someone you're not designed to be. Perhaps your father may have pressured you to be something like a jock, but your God-identity is to be a pleasant gentleman. This goes for male or female, a pessimistic mindset forms when you're expecting the worst possible outcome rather than the best possible outcome, no matter the circumstance.

It's sad to say, but one of the most common seeds of rejection are planted from the fathers who didn't show up for us when we expected him to. Maybe he didn't show up at your cheerleading competitions. He probably wasn't around for your basketball games. He didn't protect you when his wife was abusing you. Or maybe he wasn't there for your birthday. Perhaps he was not present at all throughout your entire life. So, you're left with a community of rejection within your soul.

All of the memories of your past and present emotions of rejection have caused you to believe that you're unqualified to live the best version of yourself. I believe that you've come across this book for a reason. Lord knows healing is needed because you feel this knot in your stomach as a sign that you've got some stuff festering in your soul that need to come out. Now is the time for you to break these cycles so that the relationships that God has blessed you with are no longer hindered. God truly wants to bless you with healthy relationships, unending friendships, and divine connections. He wants you to grow out of the old sins and emotional suffocations that you were born into, so that you can live in the abundance of life He's promised to birth through you.

This longing that I've carried to heal from brokenness has led me to discover a 5-step mechanism to help you heal from the cycle broken relationships and rejection. Launch into your healing by practicing these steps for *every* experience where you've felt rejected. Get your journal and a pen. Write down these experiences and follow the steps listed below. I recommend you to get into a quiet place during this exercise so that you can practice hearing from God.

1. Acknowledge Your Pain

Take a moment to think about an experience where you've felt rejected. Be honest with yourself. Don't run away from the memory. It is important that you acknowledge the pain, to confess its existence. Especially if it still bothers you.

2. Forgive and Receive

When it comes to healing from broken relationships and rejection, it is important that you seek God in the area of forgiveness. You may need to either forgive yourself or forgive someone else. Forgive yourself for getting out of character. Forgive yourself for stepping outside of God's will. Forgive the other person for causing you pain. Listen to God's guiding in both areas. He understands your imperfections. But He also would want you to acknowledge any damage that you've caused towards someone else. This is a moment where you can release yourself from feeling any weight of guilt, shame, or embarrassment. Let God know everything about how you're feeling towards the experience. Receive His forgiveness.

3. Journal the Entire Experience.

Thoroughly write what happened during the experience. How did she/he make you feel? How do you feel about it now? Remember, if it still bothers you, then you're not over the situation. Write down details as if you're talking to God. You can tell him you feel angry and frustrated. Lay it all down at the cross. Know that He is with you in this very moment. He's listening to your heart.

The art of writing your problems out to God gives you the opportunity to lay them all down at the altar. There is a release that you feel when you express your heart to God. I've had plenty of moments where I've written my heart out to God. He answers and resolves my problems every time. I'm believing that He will do the same for you too.

4. Listen for God's Response.

After writing down your experience, listen to what God is saying. You know the truth because the Holy Spirit who knows all truth lives within you. So, don't hesitate when you sense God's love guiding you through your healing process. You may feel convicted or led to remove items serving as remnant figures from your past. You may be led to listen to a song or hear a word, a phrase, or a feeling of peace flowing within you. If you feel a little lost, activate God's response by praying this prayer:

Father God, I come to you boldly with an open heart seeking to be healed from the root of rejection. John 6:63 states that it is the Spirit who gives life; the flesh profits nothing. The words that You speak to me are Spirit and life. So Lord, speak spirit and life to me so that I may hear your response to my situation. In Jesus' name, Amen.

Write down everything you sense in your spirit in this very moment.

5. Affirm God's Love Over You

After all, your heart needs a renewal of the love of God. Search scripture regarding God's love. Speak those scriptures aloud. Meditate on them daily. Write about what God is saying to you within that scripture.

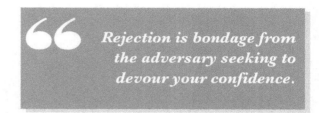

Rejection is bondage from the adversary seeking to devour your confidence.

Daily Maintenance

Defeat the spirit of rejection by affirming God's Word within your mind. Every day when you spend time with God, speak scriptures and the I...Am Biblical Affirmations over yourself as a reminder of your identity in God. One of my personal I...Am Affirmations that I speak daily is: *I am a producer of healthy relationships (from Philippians 2:2-5)*. Since speaking this affirmation over my life, I've noticed a beautiful shift in the new friendships that God has brought into my life. You can use my affirmation or get creative and come up with your own affirmations. Allow the affirmations and scriptures to flow organically.

Arnesjah Miller

I...Am Perfectly Imperfect

Breaking Loose from the Expectations of Man

Philippians 3:13 NKJV

Not that I have already attained, or am already perfected; but I press on, that I may lay hold of that for which Christ Jesus has also laid hold of me.

128

For the individual struggling to answer their calling due to their lack of perfection, can I talk to you for just a moment? Have you ever told God "no" because of your fear of man's opinions, unmet expectations, uncertainty, pride, rebellion, comfortability, or frustration? I've had to repent and surrender in this area of my life. Walking out my purpose has truly been a heavy cross to carry. I fight to maintain my sanity some days. But I wouldn't trade it for nothing. It's all worth it for the Lord.

One of my greatest fears of stepping fully into my calling is the fear of not having my life in perfect order. I recognize that I can be a little perfectionistic in most areas of my life. I work in a spirit of excellence. I've worked jobs that required me to be tedious, clean, and guarded. It's in my nature to believe that I must achieve a certain level of faith in God to pursue ministry. I reread text messages to ensure I sound gentle rather than harsh. I double check my car door to make sure it's locked. I thoroughly clean my apartment every week. I like spotless settings. I can be a handful of difficulty. With that being said, I totally understand when you think you must have it all together to pursue your purpose.

I want to take the weight of perfectionism and fear off of your shoulders. Guess what. You don't have to have it all together. You don't even have to hang onto the expectations of man. Would you like to know who God uses the most in His kingdom? The imperfect chosen ones.

But God hath chosen the foolish things of the world to confound the wise; and God hath chosen the weak things of the world to confound the things which are mighty;
1 Corinthians 1:27 KJV

Of course, there is a firm foundation of Biblical principles is prevalent to your calling. Jesus must be the epicenter of your heart before you share the gospel. You will need a prayer life to commune with the Father. A healthy perspective and a fruitful spirit are necessary. Your relationship with God is most of all important as you take on a form of leadership. A heart of humility must be evident. You never want to lead God's people astray. The love of God must reside in your heart as you minister to others. Without love, ministry is ineffective. Healing and wholeness are like medicine for the soul. You can live upon all of these qualities and still be flawed. There's no one on God's green earth that doesn't struggle with at least the smallest flaw.

We live in a society where perfectly painted pictures are portrayed at our finger tips. We get caught up in the comparison game because we haven't reached a certain plateau we've imagined. This is a dangerous trap to get stuck in. Let me tell you, beloved, the people that you see on your social media timelines are just as human as you are. They have flaws. Some have insecurities, doubts, fears, frustrations, or some problem that they don't publicly broadcast. In essence, they've reached their level of achievement because they've answered the call to pursue their purpose.

Trust me hunny, it's not easy climbing out of bed on the days defeat is knocking at your door. You've gotta put your pedal to the metal and push that dog on purpose out of you. It feels heavy. It feels uncomfortable. It seems unusual. But it is a special place built just for you. Once God qualifies you and confirms the time and moment to step into a higher level of your purpose, you must receive it. Embrace your God-identity. Accept that you powerfully impact the Kingdom of God. The worse place to be is outside of God's divine will. The beauty in all of this is that God chose you, even though you are perfectly imperfect.

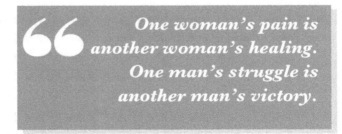

One woman's pain is another woman's healing. One man's struggle is another man's victory.

Handling Imperfect People

I truly pray you've received the healing of our Heavenly Father. You're no longer a victim to pain. You are a victor to your purpose. The imperfect people that God has placed in your life is there for you to love. They are in your life for you to give testimony of how God healed you.

It's humbling to learn how we are all imperfect. We all need prayer and healing. Many know me as a deep thinker. I am highly sensitive to spirits to point where I can observe someone and discern their issues. I even have moments where I can sit in a room and pick up on the emotions in the atmosphere. But wait, it gets even more unusual. God often times reveal to me what spirit a person is dealing with.

For instance, if God tells me that a particular friend battles with the spirit of lust, it would suddenly be confirmed by the person admitting that they deal with some form of lust. I often keep the revelation to myself and pray about it until it becomes heavy on my heart to talk to them about it. I've encountered moments where a friend made slick, side-hearted comments about my ideas. I didn't retaliate about it. I prayed against the spirit of jealousy and for her to grow in confidence. Another friend said she felt compelled to bless me. However, I noticed resentment in her heart when I couldn't afford to return the favor. I prayed against the spirit of selfishness and for her maturity. I had a friend who manipulated me countless times, after God had actually exposed her. I selflessly prayed healing over the both of our hearts. It's sad to say that talking to my friends about an issue I've noticed within them is like walking on egg shells. I get a lot of backlash and dishonesty from them even though I try to be gentle about it. I mean, is it not normal to cover a friend's flaws? Or correct a friend when they're wrong? Do we not believe in covering each other's back anymore? I've learned that when one is offended by an exposed flaw, it's not the person retaliating. It's the spirit manifesting itself due to exposure.

In the effort to cease the cycle of broken friendships, God has revealed to me the significance of categorizing friendships. You obtain peace in knowing who to set expectations for and who not to. There is so much freedom in this method! It prophetically serves as an eye-opener to who is in your life for specific reasons and seasons.

Listed below are The Ships of Relationships. There are categories that God gave me during my personal time with Him. I've developed them after receiving revelation from Lysa TerKeurst's book *Uninvited*. It's such a good read! In one of her chapters, she mentions,

"We must respect ourselves enough to break the pattern of placing unrealistic expectations on others. After all, people will not respect us more than we respect ourselves." (page 45)

Lysa's quote was such an eye-opener for me. Little did I know that I was setting unrealistic expectations on some of the relationships in my life. I was mistakenly expecting support from friends who were only placed in my life for me to pour into them.

The Ships of Relationships

Godship (Divine Relationships)
Similarity: Paul's evangelism with the 8 churches

Quite often do people come as divine encounters. It feels as like a lifetime relationship, but can end up being temporary. It is good to connect in the moment; to learn, grow, and embrace each other. But do not feel hurt or rejected when the time is over. These people were sent by God to help you to improve in your current season. Like the saying, "People come into our lives for reasons and seasons." They were sent to walk you through your current season, to help you reach your next level. Set minor expectations. Ones that will not require a heavy load to bare or solve all of your problems.

Companionship (Intimate Relationships)
Similarity: Abraham and Sarah's relationship

Closely knit relationships. You know each other's dreams and aspirations. You trust your spouse to have your back. You share similar points of views. You pray with each other and spend quality time with each other. You share a love connection with this person. Set high expectations in this relationship due to the large investment sown into each other.

Courtship (Dating Relationship)

Similarity: Isaac's relationship with Rebekah before they married (Genesis 24)

This is the time in a relationship to look forward to marriage. You're developing an intimate relationship. You hold this person accountable for knowing you on a personal level. Have high expectations with trusting you two will be married. This individual is a long-term Divine Godship.

Acquaintanceship (Temporary Relationships)

Similarity: The crowds of people that Jesus would see in passing.

People who you see regularly. You often have small conversation. You have something in common with them. You may never reach a companionship, yet both you and your friend are okay with that. It is wise to not hold any expectations for them to meet your greatest needs. There is not a large responsibility in this relationship.

Mentorship (Guidance-Oriented Relationships)

Similarity: Elijah and Elisha's relationship.

A mentee that you are setting a positive example for. One whom you are leading in the right direction. Do not hold high expectations of them to give anything in return to help your personal development. Instead, you hold high expectations for them to develop from what you are teaching them. This category is not always a life-time relationship, but could likely lead to one. This category's explanation also applies to a mentor who is guiding you.

Headship (Leader Relationship)

Similarity: Jesus' leadership with His disciples/apostles and the crowds.

Someone has the authority to lead you and a group of people for the sake of a mission. This is a leadership role. Have the expectation of the Headship to possess leadership qualities. Godly counsel is expected. You may see the formal and the informal parts of this individual's life. Do not hold expectations for this person to meet all of your needs. He/She can only give as assigned and instructed to give.

Friendship (Frequent Communication)
Similarity: Jesus's 12 disciples.
This is a very broad category. These are friends who you can depend on to help you, talk with you, and even share some secrets with. Though you may not see/speak to them every day, each time you connect, the feeling is positive and mutual. You still have expectations for this individual to meet your needs because you both have invested in each other's time. You'd expect them to attend certain events that could benefit the both of your relationship. Do not hold expectations for all friendships to pour back into you in the same amount that you pour into them because not all friends are on the same level as you. Freely give and freely receive. Friendships have a great purpose in your life.

Fanship (Follower Relationship)
Similarity: The crowds of people who deeply admired Jesus.
A Fanship is an ardent admirer or enthusiast. These are virtual or long-distant relationships and followers who admire you. They are not people who you will be closely knit with. However, you share similar qualities, interests, and understanding. They love you and the work you produce. Do not hold high expectations for this group of people. You are in their lives to pour into them. So, don't expect them to pour into you mutually.

God gave me such a peace that surpassed my understanding when I prayed over my friendships and allowed Him to help me categorize them all; to help set realistic expectations on others, not unrealistic expectations. I encourage you to pray over these categories and ask God to prophetically speak to you regarding your relationships. If He gives you more categories than what I've listed, don't hesitate to jot them down. Categorizing friendships is by no means meant to criticize anyone. It's for you to have a clear understanding of people's purpose in your life. That way you won't feel heartbroken when someone doesn't meet a standard that you were hoping they'd fulfill. We are all perfectly imperfect beings

I…Am a Child of God
Resembling God's Nature

Galatians 3:26-29 NLT

For you are all children of God through faith in Christ Jesus. And all who have been united with Christ in baptism have put on Christ, like putting on new clothes. There is no longer Jew or Gentile, slave or free, male and female. For you are all one in Christ Jesus. And now that you belong to Christ, you are the true children of Abraham. You are his heirs, and God's promise to Abraham belongs to you.

Abba Father will always see you as His beloved child. I feel a special way when I claim that I am a child of God. It makes me feel...accepted by God. I feel chosen, wanted, cared for. I can only imagine how many people haven't heard that they too are a child of God. I wonder, how many have received that they are a child of God?

Maybe you're having a hard time receiving your identity as God's child. Can I just brag about our Heavenly Father? He is amazingly extravagant. He knows our beginning to our end. Even in those moments where you're having a hard time understanding why you're faced with spiritual attacks. He's still with you, trying to show you insight within the supernatural. He is our Provider, Sustainer, Shepherd, King. Creator of the heavens and the earth. He is our Deliverer from the sin and darkness of this world. When I thoroughly think of God, I get chills. I often sit at the Lord's feet in worship, waiting for His response to my prayers. I allow the ambience of His presence rock me back and forth as if I were cradled in His arms. He responds so silently within my soul. I feel safe in knowing that my secrets are safe with Him. His goodness is unbearable.

I want you to say this with me today:
I Am a Child of God!
Feel it...Hear it...Embrace it...You are indeed a child of God. You have special privileges as His offspring. He lives, moves, and has His being in you. He is Lord over your life. He's given you a birthright to establish His covenant with you. Everything that God has established for your destiny is already done. He knows what you are going to go through in order to align with your destiny. No matter what man does, nor what you do to run off track, God has a way of tugging on your heart to real you back into alignment of your destiny.

Romans 8:29 tells us that we were predestined to conform into the image of Jesus Christ. Let that sink in, my friend. I've read over that scripture many times. But the moment when I sought after God for a better understanding of my identity, I recognized that I'm not supposed to remain the same version of myself for the rest of my life. If I was predestined to conform to the image of Jesus, then I am to become more like God in character and spirit.

Many scriptures state transformation, or metamorphosis. A few of my favorite scriptures to stand on are:

Colossians 3:1-5 NLT - Since you have been raised to new life with Christ, set your sights on the realities of heaven, where Christ sits in the place of honor at God's right hand. Think about the things of heaven, not the things of earth. For you died to this life, and your real life is hidden with Christ in God. And when Christ, who is your life, is revealed to the whole world, you will share in all his glory. So put to death the sinful, earthly things lurking within you. Have nothing to do with sexual immorality, impurity, lust, and evil desires. Don't be greedy, for a greedy person is an idolater, worshiping the things of this world.

Colossians 3:10 NLT – Put on your new nature, and be renewed as you learn to know your Creator and become like Him.

Romans 12:2 NIV – Do not conform to the pattern of this world, but be transformed by the renewing of your mind. Then you will be able to test and approve what God's will is – his good, pleasing, and perfect will.

Resembling God's Nature

To be a child of God, you are identified as His offspring. Meaning that just as you resemble your biological mother and father, you share their mannerisms, characteristics, and even their physical features. However, your DNA is uniquely fitting just for you.

When I was a child, I shared many of my mom's features. Whenever I answered the phone, my mom's friends and some of our family members mentioned that I sounded like her. Even today, when I show people a picture of her, they tell me that we look like twins. For those who've never seen a picture of my mom, they tell me that I look like my dad. Since I've lived with my dad most of my life, I see a strong resemblance of him within my facial appearance – especially my nose. I can definitely attest that I have a strong trait of his mannerisms as well – peaceful, kind, considerate, spiritually-inclined and observant. But I also know that my mom's fierce personality comes out of me sometimes.

You see, we as a person may carry similar qualities as our parents. Yet we have our own individual personality. The point that I want to present to you is that although my biophysical nature resembles the likeness of my parents, my end goal is to become spiritually resemble the likeness of God. The same goes for you too. The Bible gives us various lessons about the characteristics of God. Consider Galatians 5:22-23 - But the Holy Spirit produces this kind of fruit in our lives: love, joy, peace, patience, kindness, goodness, faithfulness, gentleness, and self-control. God's intent for humanity is for us to become more like Him so that He may share Himself with the world.

As you learn about God, you will connect more and more to your God-identity. I believe that it is no coincidence that you are reading this book. This moment is an indication that you are walking into a season of identity discovery. Or, God may be bringing to your attention the need for redefinition of your identity. Perhaps you have an ultimate vision of your purpose, but you've become caught up in the business of life and you feel as though you desperately need to get back in alignment with your relationship with God. You feel this tug and pull to walk in purpose. You know that God has more for you than where you are currently. You feel as though you are capable of taking the next step of faith, to trust God on this wild ride of faith. You desire to learn how to elevate from the natural to the supernatural. You're tired of feeling incapable of achieving greatness. You've been battling with stronghold that seemingly prevent you from walking in your purpose. You've asked God more than once, "Why do I have to live life the hard way?" Or, "Why is everyone around me receiving breakthrough besides me?" I totally understand it all. I've been through a load of spiritual warfare that caused me to question God.

I've wanted to run far away from my calling from the east is to the west. Due to a lack of fully accepting my identity, I've questioned why God would want to use me. Being called after suffering through a lifelong battle of rejection, shame, fear, inferiority, and feeling unvalued by people, I didn't want to feel the burden of God's call. I've struggled to make healthy relationships. I've wanted to settle for average. Pursing my will was never successful. Even though I have a great amount of faith in God, I still face the challenges of having faith to believe in myself. It's that barrier that we've all struggled with in our moment of pursuit. There will always be spiritual obstacles seeking to forfeit our calling. But as children of God, we must be determined to answer the call.

What's Your Supernatural Gift?

You are predestined to conform into the image of Christ Jesus. God has gifted you with one or more forms of His power. That power is the gift, the talent that that you operate the best in. I like to call it my supernatural gift. Your supernatural gift is within your passion to fulfill God's glory within the earth. It is what others can benefit from. Think of singers, writers, speakers, authors, artist, doctors, and all of the professional expertise. The people who live in those positions successfully are gifted to do so. They are literally living in their purpose, utilizing their superpower to impact the world. I'm gifted in other areas of my life, but the gifts that I operate at my highest in are the gift of poetry, intercessory prayer, and healing. It is vital that I consistently operate in this area of life to fulfill God's will.

If you don't know your supernatural gifts, I want you to pray and ask God to reveal them to you. We're living in an era where multitudes of people are discovering their supernatural gifts to pursue their purpose. God doesn't want you to be left behind. He's created you for a purpose. It can be as simple as being known as the positive person in the room. Your purpose could be mastering motherhood and a wife. If you're a creative, discovering your purpose can seem difficult to discover at first. You may have a lengthy list of ideas but not know what to do with them. It's the way God has wired you. The best way to discover your supernatural gift is to first, recognize the gift that impacts lives the most and brings glory to God. Then, don't second-guess yourself. Yes, God can use you in the most abstract areas when you allow your supernatural gift to become your lifestyle. You will begin to receive various ways of provision and doors of opportunity when you embody your supernatural gift and fulfill your purpose.

We have the greatest example of someone who embodied his supernatural gift and fulfilled His purpose – Jesus. He possessed multiple supernatural gifts as we know. But His purpose was to bring Good News to the poor, to proclaim that captives will be released, that the blind will see, that the oppressed will be set free, and that the time of the Lord's favor has come (Luke 4:18). It was His destiny to die on the cross for all of humanity, to be crowed as King. He fulfilled His ultimate purpose when He conquered the grave. Now, all of the world is impacted by this Good News.

With all that God is presenting to you in this moment, I encourage you to discover your identity as a child of God. Live out your unique greatness so that you may leave a positive impact on lives. Be the example that could help change the world for the better. Align your life with God's will. Place God first in all that you do. Trust that He will never fail you. There is greatness attached to your birthright. For you are a child of the living God.

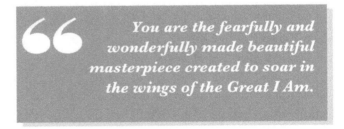

> *You are the fearfully and wonderfully made beautiful masterpiece created to soar in the wings of the Great I Am.*

I…Am Righteous
Living Out Your Faith in Christ

Romans 2:13 HCSB

For the hearers of the law are not righteous before God, but the doers of the law will be declared righteous.

What makes you righteous? Is it your works? Is it your appearance? Are you righteous based upon how well you can memorize scripture? None of these qualities make you righteous. While I've studied the book of Romans, I took my time to analyze the meaning of righteousness. I wanted to know how I am truly made righteous in God. From my studies, I've gained a clear understanding of righteousness. The biblical definition of righteousness is to be in right-standing with God. I like to think of righteousness as the counterpart to our salvation. It is a must-have characteristic of our Christian faith. Without righteousness, how can we genuinely say we are Christian? How can we truly be faithful to God if we are not in right-standing with Him? I love how the lifestyle of righteousness is stated Romans 1:17 from the Holman Christian Standard Bible:

For in (salvation) God's righteousness is revealed from faith to faith, just as it is written: The righteous will live by faith.

The righteous live by their faith (faithfulness) in Christ Jesus. I used to hear people say, "The righteous will live by faith," so many times to where I realized that I never truly dug deeper into the meaning behind that statement. This statement is expressing the spiritual principle we have life [in the spirit] when we live by our faith in Christ Jesus, and when we are faithful to God. We are made righteous when we are not only hearing the Word of God but putting the Word of God into action (Romans 2:13, emphasis added).

My search for understanding my God-identity has freed me from the prideful mentality to believe that my works alone are good enough for God. I remember when I first began ministry in the year of 2014, I was assigned to teach Sunday school, preach sermons to the church, lead in Bible Studies, evangelize in the community, and pray for people. Although I was working in the Kingdom of God, my heart was not in the right condition. Though my intentions were pure, God needed to show me deeper parts of my spirit in need of pruning. I discovered how prideful and selfish I was after a break-up from a guy I was engaged with. That painful experience then led me to realize the numerous broken women around me. Nonetheless, I needed to develop firm confidence in hearing God for myself rather than leaning on others' opinions. You see, my heart was not in healthy condition as I ministered in the pulpit, but my anointing still shined. How was this possible? It was God's grace and mercy sustaining me.

Lord knew that I was a work in progress. He knew that I had more to learn. But was I just going to sit on the sideline of inferiority because I wasn't perfectly righteous to minister? No. It wasn't my works that made me righteous. It was my faith in Christ that granted me the grace and mercy to minister the gospel. Peter didn't have it all together when He evangelized with Jesus. Paul wasn't perfect though he pursued the apostolic ministry. God knows when He is ready to send you out. He, of course, requires you to withhold a sturdy foundation of the gospel in your heart so that the deception of this world won't shake you. Your faith in Christ alone is what pleases God. He understands that you are a work in progress. Now, am I saying that it's okay to minister the gospel as you are living hypocritically against the gospel? Absolutely not! If you're struggling in tumultuous sin, you should take a seat in the pew and seek God and find a trustworthy minister to help with your deliverance.

God will always be working on your spirit, molding and shaping you to become more like Him. Nothing should hold you back from sharing the Gospel of Jesus Christ. I encourage you to renounce the doubts and fears that the enemy places in your mind. Satan seeks to devour you to prevent you from sharing this amazing Gospel that we live by. You have a story to share with others who need to know the God you serve. God takes you from faith to faith, glory to glory. Allow God to prune you in every area of your life. Always remember, it's not your work that makes you righteous, but it is your faith.

Righteousness is Purity of Heart

I want to add a kick to the expression of righteousness. I'd say that one is also made righteous by the condition of his/her heart. How is this so? Throughout scriptures, we know that our salvation in Christ Jesus is to become more like Him. A person is not of Christ if they are evil within their hearts. Nor can they become Christlike if they do not possess faith to believe He is our Lord and Savior. Without faith in God and a pure heart, one cannot see God, neither are they be declared righteous. Remember, we are righteous as we live by faith in God. I've created a visual to better express my point regarding how faith is the centerpiece of our righteousness and purity of heart.

RIGHTEOUSNESS = FAITH = PURIFICATION

Righteousness requires faith
as faith requires purity of heart.

For purification to operate in our lives, repentance must exist. Righteousness requires repentance to a certain degree. As human beings, we are bound to sin. God is very merciful in this aspect of our lives. He doesn't expect us to be perfect. However, if you know that you've sinned, it is your responsibility to get back into right-standing with God. You must acknowledge your sin, learn from it, repent, and center back on being faithful to God. Righteousness requires us to be in right-standing, or in harmony with God, and we must adhere to the law of purification.

To briefly define the law of purification, it is the discipline of spiritual holiness. When practiced consistently, one's heart manifests the qualities of God, and is transformed into the likeness of Christ within their own unique identity. For this reason, Paul included circumcision in the subject of righteousness. Romans 2:28 is where he mentioned, "For a person is not a Jew who is one outwardly, and true circumcision (purification) is not something visible in the flesh. On the contrary, a person is a Jew who is one inwardly, and **circumcision is of the heart**—by the Spirit, not the letter (law). That man's praise is not from men but from God." (HCSB)

So, what does it really mean to be righteous? To simply put it:
You are righteous because you live by faith in God through Christ Jesus.
You are righteous because you live faithfully to God's will for your life.
You are righteous because you live faithfully to God's commands and instructions.
You are righteous because you renew your mind in God's Word.
You are righteous because you live in the fruits of the Spirit.
You are righteous because you are reconciled with God.

It is so refreshing to know that because we have faith in God, we are declared righteous. There is no sin, no fear, no guilt, no shame, no lie, no demon that can take our rights away. No matter how many accusations and weapons form against us, none of them will prosper. We are covered by the blood of the Lamb. With that being said, I encourage you to own your rights. As the Bible tells us,

> *"Little children, let no one deceive you. He who practices righteousness is righteous, just as He is righteous."*
> **I John 3:7 NKJV**

I...Am an Overcomer
Becoming the Master Over Your Mind

1 John 4:4 NIV

You, dear children, are from God and have overcome them, because the one who is in you is greater than the one who is in the world.

Overcomer *n.*

A person who overcomes something: one who succeeds in dealing with or **gaining control of some problem or difficulty**; to achieve a victory over; **to master**, defeat.

The way that God wired the mind is absolutely phenomenal! We serve an extremely creative wise God! He has given you this powerful organism that controls a large percentage of your body. Then again, He has also given you a spirit that can overcome the controlling forces within your mind. I consider the brain to be the most beautiful and most powerful organ of the body. It functions in such a capacity that is beyond understanding. Scientific studies state that there is a difference between the brain and the mind. The brain is the organism. But the mind is the element. As Dr. Caroline Leaf states in her book "Switch on Your Brain," the brain is what the mind does. The dictionary defines the mind and the brain differently:

The Mind (the element)
(In a human or other conscious being) the element, part, substance, or process that reasons, thinks, feels, wills, perceives, judges, etc.

The Brain (the organism)
The brain as the center of thought, understanding, etc.; mind; intellect.

Think of it this way, the thought processes of your mind develop your brain. Like baking a cake. The result of your cake is determined upon the ingredients you placed within it. Likewise, the way you train your mind determines the functioning and development of your brain. Your mind is the environment where thoughts, ideas, emotions, and habits call home. It is the centerpiece of imagination. It is the training ground where habits develop. It is where you withhold peace. Anything can happen within your mind. The mind is always functioning to fulfill its job in keeping you alive.

The Conscious, Subconscious, and Unconscious Mind

Very briefly, I'll define and describe the mind and how it plays a role in your thought process. Sigmund Freud, a prominent neurologist and founder of psychoanalysis, described the three levels of the mind using the analogy of an iceberg. The mind is divided into three different levels: the conscious, subconscious, and the unconscious.

The conscious mind is the state of awareness where all thoughts, actions, and perceptions are defined. For example, you *learn* that giving people an encouraging word uplifts their spirit. Your conscious mind increases with the likeness of Christ as you learn more of Him.

The subconscious mind is the state of awareness where *automated reactions* are composited including memories and knowledge. For example, you meditate on scripture to improve your character. When you are tested, your automatic response is biblical instead of immature because your subconscious mind *stored* biblical principles.

Lastly, the unconscious mind is the state where we are unaware and have the most difficulty overcoming the negative emotions and thoughts that are stored within it. According to Freud's theory, the unconscious mind consists of our biologically based instincts, the primary source of human behavior. For example, responding to certain arguments with rage may feel natural to you because it resides within your instinct. No one taught you how to respond with rage, you did it unconsciously.

All three levels of your mind make up your identity in the natural. Yet, there is a supernatural newness of your identity that God desires to redefine that reflects His image. When the Bible encourages you to renew your mind, God is saying come to Him with every level of your mind. He wants to restore your thoughts, emotions, and characteristics with the likeness of Christ.

What I've come to realize is that God has not given us a mind without reason. It wasn't until I wandered into this place of discovering God on another level and developing my identity in Him that I found it necessary to reprogram my mind, literally. I've developed a firm foundation of love for Jesus. I've studied scripture based on becoming the new me in Christ. But upon entering this place of rediscovering my identity within my wilderness season, I've accepted that I cannot possess my Promised Land until I truly renew my mind. I'm talking about overcoming the mental prison of fear and breaking open the cells of limitations that have held me in bondage to thoughts of past pain. Disintegrating the shackles of poverty that have threatened to seize my prosperous future. Killing the psychedelic spirits of oppression, delusion, pride, and false assumption. This wilderness has forced me to crucify my flesh to take control of the centerpiece of my understanding. The practice of becoming the master of my mind is not easy. Although, I am taking faithful action steps daily to see the manifestation of God's promise to make me whole.

Mastering your mind is living in a mental state of overcoming. You become disciplined over your thoughts, actions, and emotions. Depending on your experience in life, you have one or more of these areas that need improvement. The mind is the battlefield. You may be dealing with traumatic experiences from your childhood, which are affecting the outcome of your life today. As a result, you've either lost all hope in obtaining a brighter future, or you're determined to overcome the thoughts of your past.

Master Your Thoughts

As you already know, God has not given you a spirit of fear and timidity, but of power, love, and a sound mind. Fear and timidity are what captivates the anxious thoughts you carry. It is the caregiver to limitations. It prevents you from believing in the possibility of change. Fear and timidity are spirits that give birth to other spirits such as insecurity, doubt, disbelief, skepticism, lackadaisicalness, lethargy, poverty, lack, and oppression. It clouds your imagination with the impossible instead of the possible.

From my personal experience with fear and timidity, I know what it's like to fight past the mental limitations that prevent victory from prevailing. I've continuously struggled with thoughts of unbelief to the point where it caused me to be oppressed from pursuing greater in life. There was a time in my life where I was given multiple opportunities to be a business owner under the help of successful mentors. Within the ages of nineteen and twenty-one, I was approached by three different women who believed I would work great as a team member of their consulting business. One woman was a Mary Kay Consultant, another woman was an Arbonne Consultant, and another woman was a Juice Plus Consultant. What's crazy is that I remember asking God for financial increase before the opportunities approached. I was just too fearful to believe in myself.

The first woman to welcome an opportunity was Mary Kay Consultant, Antoinette. She approached me while I was working at Forever 21. She told me she admired my style and thought I would be interested in an invitation to her Mary Kay makeover meeting. I prayed on the decision. I accepted the invitation. The very evening that I attended the meeting, I had become so enthused about the business that I signed up to become a Mary Kay consultant that very evening. Over time, I learned about the company. I felt welcomed and encouraged by the enthusiastic women surrounding me. Heck, even the district's independent director, Kathryn Engstrom, consistently reached out to me personally to help me succeed. I did my best to sell products. But for some reason, I kept hitting roadblocks. Of course, mental roadblocks. More like spiritual strongholds. Although I was passionate about selling Mary Kay products, I felt as though I wasn't good enough. Rejection after rejection led me to think that I was incapable of selling beauty products to women. What was also ringing loudly in the back of my mind was the thought that Mary Kay wasn't my ultimate destination. It was all I needed to quit. I was fearful of disobeying God. I always believed there was something greater upon my life.

After closing the door with Mary Kay, a few months later, I was seeking community with successful business owners to learn more about the business industry. I just so happened to come across a sweet woman who was an Arbonne Consultant, Lucille. Arbonne is a botanical beauty product and lifestyle company. Everything about the company sparked my interest, but the prices of the products were out of my league at the time. I still had a fear of man plus the fear of God ringing in my spirit. So, to save both Ms. Lucille and me the time and energy, I declined the opportunity.

A little while later, a woman who attended the same church as me welcomed the opportunity to join her Juice Plus team. I thought it would be an amazing opportunity – inexpensive, flexible, and beneficial products for both my customers and me. I did my research, purchased the products, and built my own business plan. I was confident that I could succeed in the company. Then what do ya know? I was again, struggling to overcome mental roadblocks. I was overwhelmed by fear. I was discouraged by rejection because my mind was focused on the impossible instead of the possibility of success in the experience.

Do you see the cycle of fear within my thoughts? This is exactly how fear and timidity limit the mind. Like halting at a barricade in the middle of a street, we are forced to either turn around or take a detour. Fear enforces mental roadblocks that oftentimes causes us to turn back to past thoughts of rejection, intimidation, offense, and failure. But if we don't trust in God's signs that guide us through the detour, we can end up never arriving to our destined success.

What I've learned about mastering my thoughts is that it is indeed possible to overcome fear. **You must activate your authority over fear, not allow fear to have authority over you.** I've had to acknowledge fear and push past its enforcements. I've had to decide to either go all in or go nowhere. Fear has thrown itself at me constantly during this entrepreneurial journey. I've even come across mental roadblocks while writing this book. I'd stare at the barricades of doubting people's interest in purchasing the book. I've overanalyzed my marketing strategy. I've questioned my confidence to carry out the marketing strategy successfully. But you know what I'd do after starring at the barricade? I'd look for detour signs from God. I now choose to take the unfamiliar route and trust that God is still going to lead me to my destination safely. **This is how you master the weakness of your thoughts – first, acknowledge the barricade of fear in front you.** Pray against it by renouncing it. Then, seek God's detour signs – the Word of God. Proclaim His Word over your life daily no matter circumstances. Soon enough, you will see your manifested destination.

Master Your Actions

Mastering your mind is overcoming the weakness of your actions. It is the discipline of following the will of God. It is dying to your own desires to develop the character of Christ. It is where you train yourself to trust God's voice. Have you ever been in a position where your character was challenged? If you answered no to that question, then I welcome you to Christianity, where character is one of the greatest tests of your faith.

Your actions are a big component of your mind and your heart. The treasures within your heart will either cause you to bring forth good or evil actions. That is why it is important to meditate on scripture, so that you may bring forth the characteristics of Christ. God oftentimes tests your character to reveal what is within your heart.

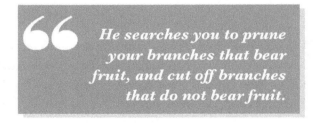

He searches you to prune your branches that bear fruit, and cut off branches that do not bear fruit.

The Lord works on your image so that you can reflect His image. I remember when my character was tested the most during a season where I was living with my dad. My character was tested while living at home with him more than dealing with the difficulties that I faced at work. One's true personality is indeed revealed within one's home. What you see in public can be a mask, but home is where the heart is. Home is the comfort of the soul.

God began to reveal to me how much anger still resided within me when He used my dad to test me. There were times where I thought the enemy was using my dad. However, I now see that God was helping me to master my actions by respecting my dad's home. It was ultimately his environment. He had his own rules. My dad graced me to live with him. He could have told me to move out long ago. Today, I still withhold the valuable lesson that God was teaching me in regards to ownership and disobedience from an argument between my dad and I. It was the pettiest thing I could have ever argued over with him.

There's this black Teflon pot that I'd always use to cook with. My dad only uses it to thaw out his frozen fish. He never uses it to cook because the Teflon at the bottom of the pot is scratched. He believes that it can cause sickness. No matter how many times I've used this particular black pot previously, it was a particular moment where my dad was compelled to tell me not to use the pot. I tried to let it go, knowing that he is a very determined man. The first time he asked me not to use the pot, I ignored him, thinking that it didn't matter. The second time he asked me, I told him I would be fine and to not make it a big deal. I proceeded to use the pot a third time. Before I began cooking with the pot, my dad confronted me.

He asked, "Why do I have to keep telling you not to use the pot?! That is my pot, and I don't want you cooking out of it! It's no good!"

I snapped back on another level, "Why are you so bothered by me using your pot! I told you it's nothing wrong with it! It's convenient for me! If the pot is no good, then I'll throw it away!" *Throws pot in the garbage can.

"Take my pot out of the garbage can! What is wrong with you?! Have you lost your mind?!" He responded.

"Well, I'm tired of you talking to me about this pot! It's nothing wrong with the pot, dad! I don't understand why you are making a big deal out of this pot!"

He proceeded, "Then, why don't you just buy your own pot instead if using mine?…"

The argument eventually ceased. I was livid. My dad was disappointed. I hadn't yelled at my dad to that degree in years. I was disappointed with myself to allow my actions to get that far out of hand. Now when I think of it, God was showing me that my dad had ownership over the pot, not me. I was operating in disobedience by ignoring my dad's rightful demand. Even if there was nothing wrong with it, I still should have respected my dad's authority. This test of my character revealed selfishness, dishonor, and disobedience that God needed to break off of me.

Is God testing your character during this season? If so, I admonish you to take heed. He could very well be trying to reveal something to you about you. If you're having trouble figuring out where God is testing you, I'll give you a little advice. Any time you are in a wilderness season, a refining period, a rediscovery season, or any time where your flesh is stretched, God is always going to uncover the real you. All that you've overcome or thought you've overcome appears again. This occurs not for you to fear again, but to improve your spiritual growth. The outcome of your character will give evidence of whether you've either mastered your actions or allowed your actions to master you.

But the fruit of the Spirit is love, joy, peace, forbearance, kindness, goodness, faithfulness, gentleness and self-control. Against such things there is no law.
Galatians 5:22-23 NIV

Your actions are symbolic of the fruit you bear. As a Christian, it is important to always bear good fruit. Bearing good fruit proves how much you dwell in secret place of the Most-High and abide in the shadow of the Almighty. It is in this dwelling place where you master your actions. The root of your actions should always be love. Because love is ultimately God's divine nature, and becoming God's nature is our mission on earth. He does everything out of love, even when He chastises you. The challenges that you face can be unpredictable and undesirable. They can even feel unbearable. Your circumstances may look like God is non-existent. You feel alone, depressed, and question God's love for you. Yet amazingly enough, all that you face is in the love of God. It is through the challenges that come in life that God brings the best out of you. He proves to you that you are stronger than you know. He reveals the depth of your understanding, the height of your victory, the greatness within you. So, don't take your present season as a loss. Count it all joy, for the testing of your faith produces endurance (patience). Let endurance have its perfect work, that you may be perfect and complete, lacking nothing (James 1:2-4 NKJV, emphasis added).

Master Your Emotions

Lastly, mastering your mind is overcoming your weary emotions - the subconscious level of your mind is where several feelings reside. The state of mind where you make good or bad decisions. Emotions fluctuate based on your senses – sight, smell, touch, hearing, taste, and thought. You can be joyful one moment. The next moment you can become upset. Your emotions change within an instant. It's the part of us where our flesh is triggered. This is completely normal within our human nature and is why it is why it a good thing to practice self-control. When you practice self-control, you have authority over your emotions instead your emotions having authority you.

Self-control can be quite a challenge, let's be honest. We are naturally inclined to desire our own way. Following God's will can be uncomfortable at times. But God teaches us how to master our emotions through our discomfort. For instance, you know those moments when you're fasting and you think about eating something or doing something that you're abstaining from? Those are the moments when you are challenged to master your emotions. Let's say you're a foodie and a nice slice of brick fire baked pizza comes to mind while you are on a dry fast. Not only does the pizza come to mind, but you are also emotionally frustrated. Why is it that during the fast you are emotionally frustrated and think of the pizza? You weren't thinking of it before. Well, it is normal to be tempted while practicing self-control amid weakness. Side note, remember Jesus was tempted to exalt Himself after 40 days in the wilderness!

During your time of fasting, you're constantly faced with the temptation to eat the pizza. Your flesh is weak screaming, "Go eat the pizza!" While your spirit is saying, "Deny your flesh!" If you are emotionally frustrated while your flesh is weak and you're allowing yourself to fantasize over the pizza, nine times out of ten, you are likely going to eat the pizza. On the contrary, you may be emotionally frustrated while your flesh is weak, but you are determined to withstand the temptation by feeding your spirit man. This is where mastering your emotions is activated. Although you may want the pizza, your spirit is strong enough to resist the temptation.

I'll provide another example for us entrepreneurs. Let's travel back to memory lane when you first started your business. Perhaps all you had was a word from the Lord, the passion to pursue your purpose, and the starting piece of your business. Did you have droughts in your business starting off? Or was your business booming since day one? Like most entrepreneurs who start from the bottom of the map, you've experienced frustration, doubt, uncertainty. Probably even questioned if you were truly in the will of God. The beginning is always going to be rough because it is literally where you are transitioning from one side of reality to another. You must train your mind to put to death the average way of thinking to pursue a higher state of believing in order to manifest the greatness within you.

There are levels to mastering your emotions. You elevate to a point where God sees what areas you can handle. You come to a place where God can entrust you to make mature decisions. Like handling a massive amount of money, or managing a six-figure business, or leading a large community of people, or even mothering or fathering a household. Yielding to the will of God places you right where you need to be. He believes in you and He knows what you can handle in any given season.

The following questions that I am going to ask you may seem a bit challenging, but are necessary to ask yourself as you master your emotions as an entrepreneur. They are not meant to be self-inflicting, but to consider as you grow as a man or woman of God. Will you budget properly so that you can have enough funds to sustain your business? Will you fast and pray for God-ordained solutions? Will you hold your tongue when a customer or client disrespects you? Will you remain humble when people crowd you with praise? Will you continue to seek God when things are going swell for you? Will you still resemble the nature of God when the adversary tempts you in your weakest state of mind? Will you still love others with the love of Christ in spite of how you feel towards them? All of these questions are essential to take into consideration. As I've experienced all of them in my wilderness season, I've had to turn back to God to repent and ask Him to cleanse me again and again. My emotional state of mind is fragile, but I am determined to work out my own soul's salvation. God has sat me in front of some prominent people to show me good and bad examples of Godly character within leadership. I've sat amongst very few leaders that were nasty in character, yet were successful in business. Communing with them influenced me to always stay close to the heart of God. Others on the other hand, I've admired and enjoyed their fellowship.

Entrepreneurship can ruffle up some crazy emotions. In those periods when business doesn't seem to be as appeasing as you'd like, you have to continue to carry out your business. You may have to reorganize some of your strategies or pray for God to provide solutions. You may have to let some people go. But your emotions, you have to get a grip on them. When God elevates you to higher heights, He trusts that you can withstand the challenges. All of the character development that you've endured during your wilderness season will make a world worth of sense when you enter your Promised Land.

Mastering your emotions is effectual when you are in your wilderness season. The reason being is because you are naturally inclined to manage responsibility the best you know-how. God has a special unpredictable way of taking over your circumstance to show you how He provides. It feels as if you are stripped from all you know. Your mind races with thoughts of,
"How are my bills going to get paid?"
"How can I save up for my business?"
"How am I supposed to sustain myself if I don't have the funds?"
"I have responsibilities! How am I supposed to take care of my family?"
"Why can't I keep money in my account?"

All the while your mind is freaking out, God is waiting on you to silence yourself. As Proverbs 3:5-6 states, God is calling you to trust in Him with all of your heart, and lean not unto your own understanding. To acknowledge Him in all of your ways, and He will direct your steps. Worry does nothing but run your blood pressure through the roof. It creates chaos instead of peace. But in those moments when you silence your emotions, God speaks to you. He gives you direction, strategy, understanding, and peace of mind.

Master Your Mind to Become Christlike

Peace is ultimately cultivated when you master your mind. After all, peace is what all three levels of your mind seek to conquer. It is one of the many levels within success that your soul longs for. The highest level of success is to master the principle of love. How do you define success? Is it in money? Ownership? Materialism? Success is none of these things. **The highest level of success you could ever achieve is to master becoming Christlike.** This success is not easily obtained. Its cost requires a sacrifice – a lifestyle of daily surrender to our Lord. He is our example of One who mastered His mind. His level of thinking was incomparable. He brought us a new level of understanding that has changed the world forever. He embodied the principles of life. Hence, He calls us to take and eat of Him that we may have spiritual life through Him. To drink of His blood, that we may receive forgiveness of sins.

Jesus' death on the cross alone should prompt us to humbly lay our lives down to not only follow Him, but mimic Him. I know this message was lengthy. But I want you to understand how much God is seeking to get you to understand how important it is to elevate your level of thinking. We as God's people have long-lived in a place of mental captivity where we haven't fully grasped an understanding of the freedom and life that is obtained when living out the mindset of Christ Jesus. It is written that Jesus told His disciples that we will do even greater works than Him if we believed in Him. He said that He would do whatever we ask in His name (John 14:12-13, emphasis added). So, if this is true, why can't we master our mind to become more like Jesus?

Mastering your mind to become Christlike is this very scripture from
Colossians 3:1-11 (NIV):

> *Since, then, you have been raised with Christ, set your hearts on things above, where Christ is, seated at the right hand of God. Set your minds on things above, not on earthly things. For you died, and your life is now hidden with Christ in God. When Christ, who is your life, appears, then you also will appear with Him in glory. Put to death, therefore, whatever belongs to your earthly nature: sexual immorality, impurity, lust, evil desires and greed, which is idolatry. Because of these, the wrath of God is coming. You used to walk in these ways, in the life you once lived. But now you must also rid yourselves of all such things as these: anger, rage, malice, slander, and filthy language from your lips. Do not lie to each other, since you have taken off your old self with its practices and have put on the new self, which is being renewed in knowledge in the image of its Creator. Here there is no Gentile or Jew, circumcised or uncircumcised, barbarian, Scythian, slave or free, but Christ is all, and is in all.*

Mastering your mind to become Christlike is transformation from darkness to like. To become Christlike is to put to death the sin-cycles you've battled with - the lying tongue, stealing people's ideas, gossiping, arguing, pursuing lustful desires, and such actions. Becoming Christlike is walking in your purpose to operate in your God-identity. I tell you the truth, becoming Christlike may sound a bit hard to take in at the moment for you. But there comes a time when it'll be time for you to respond to God's call. No worries, though. Your spirit will respond because your inward being longs for fulfillment from the Father. With that being said, I encourage you my friend, to seek God in breaking every limit off your understanding. You have a purpose to fulfill. If you can master your mind, you can master anything.

I...Am Chosen

Confidently Embrace Your God-Identity

Esther 4:14 NIV

For if you remain silent at this time, relief and deliverance for the Jews will arise from another place, but you and your father's family will perish. And who knows but that you have come to your royal position for such a time as this?"

1 Peter 2:9 KJV

*But ye are a **chosen** generation, a royal priesthood, a holy nation, a peculiar people; that ye should shew forth the praises of him who hath called you out of darkness into his marvelous light.*

I...Am Chosen

If you have received anything out of this entire book, know that you are chosen. Being chosen can be hard to accept for some. For others, it's their committed lifestyle. I personally have experienced the struggle of embracing my calling in life – to be holy, to be set a part, to be indifferent from others, to access my peculiar identity. No matter how much I've tried to live my own way comfortably, God always reminds me of why I am called. There are people battling with spiritual suffocation, and God uses me to help bring them out. I've learned that sleeping on my calling doesn't bring me joy. Though I have the heart to help, there are days where I've tried to isolate myself to prevent myself from carrying the burdens of broken souls. I sometimes have to fight for my sanity. Most people aren't expressing the truth behind being chosen. I share my transparency with you because I want you to know that you are not alone.

Your identity as a chosen one means a lot to God. He's called you to do greater works for His glory. He never intends to forsake you, so don't ever think you have to walk this journey alone. Receive that you are loved. The love of God casts out all fear. Receive His everlasting love today, knowing that no matter what season you're walking through, God is with you. Receive that you are virtuous. Remember that virtue is an inward manifestation of God's exuberant wisdom and power. So, never settle for less than your value. Receive that you are heard. Speak up and allow your story to be told. The gifts you carry can help bring someone out of the darkness that you've been through. Receive that you are victorious. You overcome the darkness of this world by your faith in Jesus. There is nothing that you cannot do, for greater is God within you than he that is in the world.

Receive your creative instinct. With all the abundant ideas that God has flowing through you, utilize that power to express the glorious wonders of God. Renounce suicidal thoughts! The enemy will not tear you apart! What's inside of you must come out of you! God is not done with you yet! Receive that you are innovative. You have the ability to develop new strategies that yield a harvest of abundance. Receive that you are favored. Renew your mind and stop limiting your blessings. God desires to favor you in all that you do for His Kingdom. Receive that you were created to be fearless. God has not given you the spirit of fear and timidity, but of power, love, and a sound mind.

Be transformed by the renewing of your mind daily by renouncing every fear that is holding you back from becoming the greater version of you.

Beloved, receive that you are indeed FREE! Jesus has already established your freedom from sin. It is in your thinking and doing that you must practice the discipline to no longer allow yourself to be a victim to sin. Receive that you are powerful. Unlock your God-Given power and explode with the glory of God in your calling. As you embrace who you are, proclaim that every mountain be moved in Jesus name! Receive that you are blessed. Come out from among every demonic interception that is blocking your blessings. Renew your mindset to defeat the spirit of poverty, lack, and depletion in the name of Jesus! Receive your newness in Christ. Make it a habit to die to your old ways so that you can flourish in a better state of mind.

Receive that you are healed, my friend. You know longer have to carry the wounds of the past. Give your pain and sorrow to Jesus so that you can minister healthy and effectively to those in need. Receive that you are forgiven. Release yourself from every weight of shame, fear, and condemnation. You are not a mistake. Even if you make mistakes, God is not holding it against you. Your sins are forgiven. Receive that you are not rejected. Be healed, in Jesus' name, from every area of brokenness in your life. Receive that you are perfectly imperfect. You don't have to have it all together to be accepted by God. Recognize the friends and acquaintances in your life, categorize them, and be free from the expectation of man.

Receive that you are a child of God. Wrap your mind around the simple truth that He cares for you. Take on the resemblance of God as you discover more of your identity in Christ. Receive that you are righteous. Remember all the rights that you own as a child of God. Live out your faith in Christ, for your faith is what makes you righteous. Above all, receive that you are chosen by God, created to do greater works for His kingdom.

How do you feel after receiving these heavenly treasures? May you receive every good and perfect gift that comes from above. It is my prayer that you find growth, strength, healing, and the embrace the love of God that has set you free. I encourage you to not only to hear or read what has been given to you. But put into action the workings of God. Consistently speak the living Word of God your life daily. You have a mission to fulfill, and God has a promise to give. Now, go and confidently embrace your God-identity.

Arnesjah Miller

I...Am

Original Spoken Word Poem from Transparent Treasure:
My Darkness Turned into Light

I...Am,
Not what others perceive me to be.
What creates my image,
Is the Spirit of God
Residing in me.

For I...Am,
More than dust in the wind.
The pottery of my skin
Is more valuable than
Man-made's materialistic perfection.

Words can never be too tough
To tear my integumentary.
Fear is no longer a fossil
Embroidered in my mentality.

For I...Am,
An engraved image given life.
Once dead, but now a light.
Created to restore hidden treasure.
Formed to know more about my Creator
Who told me that -

I...Am,
An opportunity.
A chosen one of God-given royalty.
Worth more than the fight for freedom and justice.
Unlike liberty I am given a promise.

I...Am Chosen

I'm called bring a unique peace.
Not the piece of riots and chaos seen on the streets.
But in corners unseen,
I put in time.
For God I live, for Christ I die.

For God, I...Am,
Developing His purpose.
Walking a voyage with faith
In the world unseen.
Even through the trials and tribulations,
I can say that I, believe.

I believe that even though I lack perfection,
I am still a masterpiece to God.
I believe that even when I'm not accepted,
I know this is where I belong.
The identity of my heart is given
Because of God who exists
In the blood of my art.

Daily, I am reminded that
Survival isn't an option.
I refuse to fall to the waist-side
And drown in a dam with society.
I refuse to believe that good health
Is expensive and good wealth is earthly.

Lord knows that in this world only,
Am I thriving to live my life filled with wisdom.
Am I seeking higher dimensions.
Am I living amongst twisted lies from ongoing generations.
Am I running nonstop towards my destination.

In this world only,
Have I not given up on breaking the chains of slavery;
Fighting against oppositions of the truth.
Fighting past my blind side to get a breakthrough.
Fighting for the harvest that my ancestors strived to reap.
And yet I'm trying to get past the fact that
I...Am, not fighting against flesh and blood.
But against the evil authorities
Of spiritual forces within this dark world only.

I...Am,
Running off of Rivers of Living Water;
Seeking God as my Provider.
To fill the cups of the thirsty,
Feed the minds of the hungry,
Light up like electricity,
Reach my destiny,
Leave a legacy,
And pursue the purpose
That THE GREAT I AM PROMISED ME...

Because after all,
In this world only,
Life has proven to me
That I...Am,
Not at home...
And I won't be.
Until my portrait is complete
In the eyes of God,
I...Am.

I…Am Chosen

About the Author

As a Poet and Entrepreneur, Arnesjah is an aesthetically diverse individual who seeks to make a positive impact on lives. After growing up with a challenging childhood, Arnesjah saw the need of a positive change in the world and developed a desire to lead others into pursuing their God-given purpose. Today, she lives by example to help transform lives for the better through ministering poetry. Her poetry is known to impact lives. She is noticed as a peace-maker, a light in a room.

Since the age of 18, Arnesjah has ministered poetry on various occasions at community events, churches, and open mics. She has co-lead on the Prayer Team at a prominent church and enjoys learning about the prophetic. She believes in the freedom of Christ and possesses a heart to see others live in that freedom. Therefore, she welcomes everyone to join the journey in shining forth the marvelous light of God. She takes delight in her business, Prayer Mats by Arnesjah, where she creates hand-crafted Prayer Mats for comfortability, inspiration, and power in prayer. You can find out more information about Prayer Mats by Arnesjah at www.prayermatsbyarnesjah.com. To find more information about Arnesjah visit www.transparenttreasure.com.

NOTES

Freud, S. (1915). *The Unconscious* (Vol. 6). (P. Rieff, Ed.) New York, United States: Collier Books Macmillan Publishing Company.

Kismet, M. (2018). Psychological Effects of Growing Up Without a Father. *Owlcation*.

McLeod, S. (2009, 2015). Unconscious Mind. *Simply Psychology*.

Tracy, B. (n.d.). The Power of Your Subconscious Mind. *Brian Tracy International*.

Made in USA - Kendallville, IN
1168246_9781713095019